Volume 5
of fifteen volumes

HOLIDAYS AND CUSTOMS

CHILDCRAFT

The How and Why Library

FIELD ENTERPRISES EDUCATIONAL CORPORATION
CHICAGO
LONDON • ROME • STOCKHOLM • SYDNEY • TORONTO

Acknowledgments

The publishers of CHILDCRAFT—THE HOW AND WHY LIBRARY gratefully acknowledge the following publisher and organizations for permission to use copyrighted illustrations. Full illustration acknowledgments for this volume appear on pages 362–363.

California Institute of Technology and Carnegie Institution of Washington: page 185

Curtis Publishing Co.: painting by Ludwig Bemelmans, page 260, reproduced by permission from *Holiday* Magazine, copyright 1961 by Curtis Publishing Co.

CONTENTS

VOLUME 5 *Holidays and Customs*

HOLIDAYS AND CUSTOMS

Everywhere in the world a holiday is a special time to celebrate. If you take the word "holiday" apart, you have two words, "holi" and "day," or holy day. Long ago, all holidays were days for celebrating something holy. But now, holidays are days for celebrating other things, too.

A holiday may last just for a day, like Thanksgiving Day. Or it may last for many days, like the holidays at Mardi Gras.

For children, a holiday can mean no school! For grownups, it can mean time off from work.

Some holidays are for honoring a special person, or for remembering something that happened long ago. Other holidays are for worship, and some are just for play and having fun.

People in all parts of the world celebrate their holidays in special ways that they call customs. A custom is something that people do over and over, just as their fathers and grandfathers did. But customs are not just for holidays. Customs are part of everyday life, too. The way you eat is a custom and so is the way you dress.

Now you can find out about different customs that people of many lands have at holiday times and in their everyday lives.

4

COSTUMES FOR
SPECIAL DAYS

There are days
to dress like giants
and days to put on bread,
and days to wear an onion
right upon your head!

There are days
to put on masks or feathers,
to dress up like a clown,
to carry bells or dragons,
or candles in a crown.

On these pages
you can find out
about special days
for putting on costumes.

Mardi Gras

At the Mardi Gras carnival in New Orleans, Louisiana,
you see people in costumes and masks that make them look
   like famous people of long ago,
   like characters in a storybook,
   like witches and clowns and devils,
   like creatures from the sea.
You see a King of the Carnival, too.
He parades in a white silk costume,
and he carries a golden sword and a golden staff.

In many other parts of the world,
people have carnivals
like the one in New Orleans before Lent begins.

candle crowns

How would you like to wear candles on your head?

You may if you go with the grownups and the children
who parade with lighted candles in their hats
on Santa Claus Night in Switzerland.

Your hat is not an ordinary hat.
It is a big one, made of cardboard and colored silk.
A candle burns inside and makes it glow in the dark.
Because your hat is so big, it will not catch on fire.

When you wear one of these hats on Santa Claus Night,
you are called a Klause.
Along with the other boys and girls,
you follow Santa Claus when he comes to town
on the night of December 6.

If you are a girl who lives in Sweden,
you may wear lighted candles in a crown.
You are the Lucia Queen,
and you wear your crown of candles on Saint Lucia's Day,
the 13th of December.
Early in the morning you put on your crown
and go through the house
waking up your family with songs and food.

　SANTA CLAUS AND FATHER CHRISTMAS　　　　PÈRE NOËL

Which one is Santa Claus?

SAINT NICHOLAS

They ALL are.
They wear different clothes,
and they have different names,
but they are all Santa Claus—
in different lands.

In the United States,
you know that Santa Claus
wears a bright red suit
trimmed with white fur,
a long red cap,
and shiny black boots.
In England, he wears
the very same outfit,
but there he is called
Father Christmas.

In France, he is called Père Noël,
which means Father Christmas.
But he doesn't look a bit like
the Father Christmas of England.
Père Noël is tall and skinny.
He wears a long red robe
and a white fur hat,
and he clatters along
in wooden shoes.

In Switzerland you see
still another Santa Claus.
He wears the clothing of a bishop—
long white robes
and a tall, pointed hat
called a miter.
His name is Saint Nicholas.

INDIAN

"See you at the Pow-Wow."
That is what Indian boys and girls
in the United States say to each other
for months before the Fourth-of-July weekend.

The boys polish their great-grandfathers' tomahawks.
They paint new feathers to wear in their hair.
They clean their wampum beads to wear around their necks.
And they shine their best silver and copper jewelry.

Children of twenty great Indian tribes—
Apache, Hopi, Zuñi, Navajo, and others—
gather together in Flagstaff, Arizona,
for one great Pow-Wow celebration.

For three days, dressed in their finest costumes,
they have parades, rodeos, war dances, and snake dances.
Only real Indians can take part in the great Pow-Wow,
but everyone can watch.

POW-WOW

witches,
goblins,
and
ghosts

On Halloween, you put on a scary mask so that no one can tell who you are. You dress up to look like a witch, a black cat, a goblin, a skeleton, or a ghost—and all because years ago people thought that ghosts roamed the earth at night on Halloween, the 31st of October.

In Austria, you wear your scary mask at carnival time, just before Ash Wednesday. You and your friends run around beating drums, dancing, ringing bells, and making as much noise as you can. People in Austria say that scary animals and witches will scare away the winter.

THE NEW YEAR'S
Dragon

Here comes the dragon!
Its mouth is open,
and its bright red tongue is sticking out.
Its horns are silver,
its beard is green,
and its eyes are gold and blue.
It is a scary dragon, but it isn't real.
It is part of a Chinese New Year parade.

Inside the dragon are men and boys who carry it
as they zigzag their way through the streets.
They hop and jump and weave in and out—
and so does the dragon!

parade of GIANTS

Imagine a parade of giants
on their way to a wedding!
One of the giants is dressed as a bride.
She is about to be married
to a giant called Goliath.
Goliath is dressed in armor from head to foot,
and he carries a mighty club.
Other giants have come to the wedding, too!
One is named Samson.
He carries part of a broken temple.
Another is named Miss Victory.
She wears a great cape and a golden crown.

Every August you see these giants on parade
in a little town in Belgium.
The giants are make-believe,
but they look almost real.
A man walks inside each one.
When you watch the parade,
you cannot see the man.
He can see you, though,
because he has a peephole in front
so that he can see where he is going.

onions
that
walk

Did you ever see an onion walking?
You may think so if you are in Switzerland
when the Onion Market opens in November.
That is when a parade of onions
marches in the public square.
The onions have funny faces painted on them.
Some are smiling.
Some are frowning.
Some even have mustaches!

But these are not real onions.
Onions are never that big,
and who ever saw an onion smile?
They are really men
carrying great big onion heads
made of paper and cloth.

mummers

on parade

In one parade you see thousands of people dressed in fantastic costumes. They look like

spacemen, hoboes, clowns,
kings in royal robes,
queens in fancy silks,
Indians, African warriors,
and almost anything else.

The people in the parade are called mummers. They march every year on New Year's Day in Philadelphia, Pennsylvania. To welcome in the New Year, the mummers sing, dance, and play tricks as they parade through the streets. Judges watch the parade and give prizes for the best and most interesting costumes.

wearing of the

In New York City
on St. Patrick's Day
you see a big parade
of people dressed in green.
The people are parading
in honor of Saint Patrick,
who died long ago
on March 17 in Ireland.
Irish people in Philadelphia,
Boston, and many other cities
also march in costume parades
on St. Patrick's Day.

The reason everyone wears green
is that green is supposed to be
Ireland's favorite color.
Nearly everything
the marchers wear is green!—
their hats, their trousers,
their coats, their ties,
and their socks.
They carry green flags,
and they even wear
a little green three-leaf clover
called a shamrock.

If they are lucky enough
to own one, they also carry
a special walking stick
called a shillelagh.
(You can pronounce it
by saying "shill-LAY-lee.")

GREEN

27

Carnival of the Gilles

Nearly everyone wants to be a gille
when it's Carnival of the Gilles time,
just before Lent begins.

If you are a gille,
you get to wear a marvelous costume.
For three days and three nights,
you dance, sing, and parade
through the streets.

The word gille
means clown in French,
but a gille
is a special kind of clown.
He wears a big tall hat
with feathers of many colors,
bell-bottomed trousers
trimmed with fancy lace,
a golden collar
with tinkling bells,
and heavy wooden shoes.

Gilles carry baskets of oranges,
and as they dance,
they throw oranges into the crowd.

It is a lot of fun to be a gille,
but the only place in the world
where you can be a gille
is in the town of Binche in Belgium.

BREAD
ON
YOUR
HEAD

You've seen people wearing hats. But have you ever seen anyone wearing a hat made of piles of bread and flowers? You may if you are in Portugal in July for the Festival of the Trays. You see six hundred girls wearing enormous hats that are as tall as they are.

Each hat is a tray. On each tray is a basket made of wire and bamboo sticks. The wire and sticks hold up a tower of bread and colored flowers. On top of this tower of bread sits a white dove made of cotton.

The girls parade into the city square where the bread on their heads is blessed. Then they give the bread to the poor.

This festival is so old that nobody remembers when or how it started, but the people in Portugal say that it is a time to give thanks for having bread and food for all.

Bells on Their Backs

Can you imagine having to run through the streets with a bell on your back? If you are a carnival runner in a small town in Switzerland, that is how you ring in the spring when winter is almost over.

You put on a grotesque mask made out of wood, and tie a bell on your back—you might even tie another bell in front of you! And you might wear a big, funny hat with dolls and flowers on it. Then, ringing and clanging, you run through the streets for three days and three nights, just before Lent begins.

CLOTHES IN MANY LANDS

What a surprise it might be
to look into your closet
and suddenly find
a hat made of bamboo,
a skirt made of leaves,
trousers made of sheepskin,
and shoes made of wood.

Where in the world
would you wear such clothes?

Here you can find out
about some of the clothes
that people wear
in different parts of the world.

IF YOU WERE A HAT

If you were a hat,
what would you like to do?

Would you like to cover a heart?
When soldiers and sailors salute
their country's flag,
they keep their hats on.
But most other men
take off their hats
and cover their hearts with them.

If you were a hat,
would you like to sail through the air?
Students at military school
take their hats off
and throw them high
on graduation day.

If you were a hat,
would you like to be part of a bullfight?
When a bullfighter
is ready to finish his bullfight,
he takes off his black hat
and throws it to the person
in whose honor the bull is killed.

Look at all the hats in this window! Why don't you try on a few?

A high hat made of monkey fur may look as fine on you as it does on a tribal chieftain in Kenya, Africa.

Here is a hat that stands even taller. It is a tower of lace that women wear in a part of France called Brittany.

If you don't care for lace, you might prefer a hat made of bamboo. It is the hat that farmers in Thailand wear.

Instead of a stiff and hard bamboo hat, try on this soft little beret. You might see a beret in almost any country.

Another small hat is the mortarboard cap. A college graduate wears this cap on the day that he is graduated.

But if you really want to have fun, wear the hat that looks like part of a monstrous bull. Some people in Africa wear this hat when they do special dances.

Even your own hat might look strange to people in other lands.

A WORLD OF HATS

MONKEY-FUR HAT

LACE HAT

BAMBOO HAT

BULL-HORN HAT

BERET

MORTARBOARD

37

clothes picked from trees

On a rainy day in Argentina,
you might see some trees walking.
But when the trees get closer,
you see that they're really not trees at all.
They're people wearing
rain capes made from leaves
that are as big as elephant ears.

Girls in Hawaii sometimes wear leaves, too.
The leaves are called ti leaves.
The girls use them to make
the grass skirts they wear
when they dance a hula.

The grass skirts of some women
in the Pacific Islands
are short and bushy.
These skirts are made with
leaves from coconut trees.

MONGOLIA

VIETNAM

WHO WEARS

There is no rule that says:
ALL WOMEN MUST WEAR DRESSES.
ALL MEN MUST WEAR TROUSERS.
In some countries,
people dress just the other way around.

In Mongolia,
women wear trousers made of sheepskin.
People there don't think it odd
to see girls in baggy trousers.
If the girls wore dresses,
how could they ride their horses so fast?

Women in a country called Vietnam
wear dresses and trousers
at the same time.
They put on their dresses
over trousers that they call cuans.

40

MALAYA　　　　　　　　SCOTLAND　　　　　　　　GREECE

WHAT?

Men in Scotland sometimes
wear skirts called kilts.
Besides wearing skirts,
they even have purses!
The purses, or sporrans,
are made of fur,
and they hang from a belt
on the kilt.

Skirts are also clothes for both men
and women in Malaya.
Their skirts are called sarongs.
Sarongs are made from cotton or silk.

Men called evzones,
of the Greek Royal Guard,
wear skirts when they guard
the Royal Palace in Athens.

41

42   INDIA   SPAIN

TWIST YOUR CLOTHES

In some places you wind yourself into and out of your clothes.

Women in India make dresses called saris. A sari is a long piece of cloth that a woman wraps around herself. With the loose end of the sari she makes a shawl to cover her head.

A Spanish goatherd knows a quick way to make a cloak. He wraps a blanket around his shoulders. Then he is ready to sit outdoors and watch his goats.

In parts of India and Africa, men make their own hats every day. Their hats are called turbans. Turbans look like towels that the men wind around and around their heads.

INDIA

AFRICA

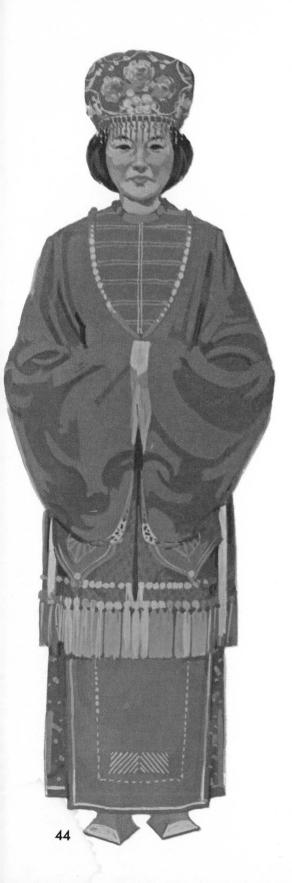

COLORS THAT SAY THINGS

You can speak with words.
But sometimes clothes
that are colorful can speak for you.

For a long time in China,
it has been a custom
for a bride to wear a
red silk gown.
Red shows that she is happy
to be married.

People who live in the South Sea Islands
put on black-and-white striped clothes
when a friend dies.
The black stripes are for sadness.
The white stripes are for hope
that the friend will go to heaven.

At many college graduations,
professors wear black robes
trimmed in colors.
Usually, the colors tell you
what subjects they teach.

Yellow may be for science.
Pink may be for music.
Blue may be for education.
Green may be for medicine.
Purple may be for law.

clothes that can be other things

In some countries, your clothes can become
other things besides clothes.

Hats can be bread trays.
In an African country called Ghana,
the women who sell loaves of bread
wear hats that look like big trays.
They put all the loaves
on top of their hats.

Hats can be buckets.
Cowboys wear "ten-gallon" hats.
When the cowboys fill them with water,
their horses can drink from these hats.

Jackets can be beds.
In Greenland, women wear jackets
with pouches on the back.
Little children can sleep
when they ride in the pouches.

Caps can be purses.
Portuguese men like to wear stocking caps.
They sometimes put coins and tobacco
inside the tips of their caps.

47

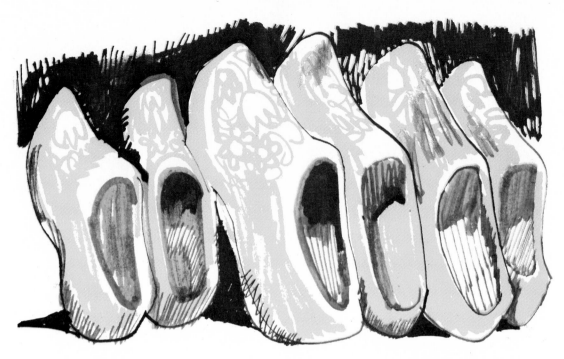

KLOMPEN IN HOLLAND

SHOES
THAT
CLATTER

GETA IN JAPAN

Boys and girls in some countries
clatter when they walk.

In Holland, Belgium, and France,
they sometimes wear wooden shoes.
In Holland they are called klompen.
In France and Belgium
they are called sabots.
It really won't matter
if the shoes splatter mud.
Feet don't get wet
in wooden shoes.

In Japan, a child can wear
a pair of wooden clogs called geta.
The clogs are raised on stilts
that keep his feet from getting wet.

The Rules for Shoes

Do you know the rules for shoes wherever you go?

In Japan, you take off your shoes before you go into the house. Otherwise you would tear the straw mats on the floor. You can even go barefoot in school.

In Holland, you might see a row of wooden shoes on the doorsteps. If Dutch people wore wooden shoes while they walked around the house, think of all the racket that the shoes of wood would make!

People who live in a country called Bhutan don't have any rules for shoes. In fact, they often don't have shoes. Instead of wearing boots when they play in the snow, they just "wear" their bare feet, and play in the snow anyway.

SHOES ON A DOORSTEP IN JAPAN

FLAGS

If you had all the flags
in the world,
you could look at them
and see pictures
of crowns, crests,
crosses, and crisscrosses,
suns, moons, stars, and stripes,
castles, curves,
circles, and swords,
and even elephants,
eagles, and bears.

Here you can find out
what people do with flags.

FLAGS FOR

On the Fourth of July in the United States,
you see flags almost everywhere you look.
You see flags on flagpoles and flags in parades,
flags on houses, flags on stores,
flags on office buildings,
and even flags on cars and bicycles.
Some flags are as small as a handkerchief.
Some flags are as big as a bedsheet.
But they all have stars in the corner
and stripes going across.
Everyone is celebrating Independence Day—
the day the United States was born.

BIRTHDAYS

Other countries celebrate their birthdays too. These are a few of them.

FRANCE

July 14 . . . Bastille Day

MEXICO

September 16 . . . Independence Day

CANADA

July 1 . . . Dominion Day

INDIA

January 26 . . . Republic Day

SOME
DAYS
FOR
FLYING FLAGS

The flags that you see flying
on some special days
are in honor of certain people,
places, and even flags.
In the United States,
people fly flags on many special days.

WASHINGTON'S BIRTHDAY—February 22
To honor the first President

LINCOLN'S BIRTHDAY–February 12
To honor the 16th President

MEMORIAL DAY—May 30
To honor people who died in wars

FLAG DAY—June 14
To honor the flag

INDEPENDENCE DAY—July 4
To honor the country's birthday

COLUMBUS DAY—October 12
To honor America's discovery

VETERANS DAY—November 11
To honor people who were in wars

ONE FLAG

You know that every country has a flag. But do you know that some flags stand for many countries?

At the Olympic Games, where people from many lands have contests, you see the Olympic Flag. It is white, and it has five rings in the middle. The rings are blue, yellow, black, green, and red. You can see at least one of these colors in every flag in the world. The rings are locked together to show the friendship of the people at the games.

for many countries

At the United Nations, you see another flag that stands for many countries. It is a flag for the people of many lands. It is a blue flag with a map of the world in the middle. On each side of the map is an olive branch. The olive branches stand for peace.

THE FLAGS I FLY

When I play with my boats,
sometimes I am a swashbuckling pirate
with a ragamuffin crew.
And I sail the salty sea
in search of buried treasure.
My flag is the Jolly Roger,
and it flutters from my highest mast
for all other ships to see.

Sometimes I am admiral of the fleet.
My ship is a battleship,
and my flag is an admiral's flag.
Everywhere I look across the sea,
there are other ships that follow me.

Sometimes I am the captain of a merchant ship,
as she plows the waves of a stormy sea
or wallows on a gentle swell.
My ship carries cargo to far-off lands,
and the flag I fly is my country's flag.

When you see a ship,
look at the flags she flies.
They can tell you where a ship is from,
where she is going,
and who owns her.

FLAGS

THAT SPELL

Do you know what these flags say?

H E L L O

If you are a sailor, you do.
They spell "Hello."

Sailors almost everywhere
know how to send messages with flags.
Some of the flags that they use
stand for the letters of the alphabet.
Some stand for numbers.
Some stand for whole words.
When you send messages
with flags like these,
you are using a code
called the International Flag Code.

Sailors also send messages
with flags they hold in their hands.
A sailor holds the flags
in different positions
to send the letters and numbers
in a message.

Fish Flags

If you are in Japan or Hawaii on May 5, you celebrate Boys Day. You see flags that look like toy fish. Each fish flag on a house stands for one boy in the family. The biggest flag is for the oldest boy. The smallest one is for the youngest boy. Families fly the flags to show that they want their boys to be brave and strong.

FIREWORKS, FIRES, AND CANDLES

Fireworks sizzle,
bang, and boom.
Fires snap, pop, and crackle.
Candles flicker and glow.

Here is how people use their
fireworks, fires,
and candles
at celebrations.

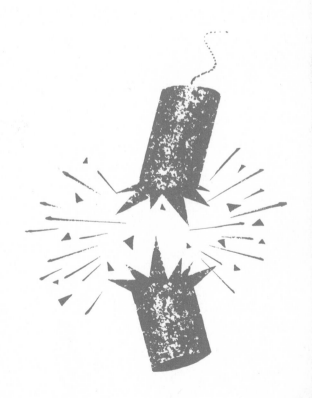

MAKE
A WISH
AND
BLOW!

One, two, three, blow!
Blow out the candles
on your birthday cake.
But don't forget to make a wish.
Some people say
that the wish will come true
if you blow out all the candles
with one big breath.

The older you are,
the more candles
you have to blow out.
Every year you get
one more candle
on your birthday cake.

Instead of blowing out
your own candles,
perhaps you can have each person
at your party make a wish
and blow out one candle.
Then, at least one wish
is sure to come true!

Mary Horton

JACK-O'-LANTERNS

When you make a jack-o'-lantern for Halloween,
you carve a funny face
or a scary face on a pumpkin
and put a candle inside it.

Did you ever wonder why you make
jack-o'-lanterns?
People of Ireland say that it is because of
a man named Jack, who lived long ago.
Jack was so stingy
that he couldn't get into heaven.
There just wasn't any place he could go.
So, he had to walk around the earth and
carry a lantern everywhere he went.
People called him "Jack of the lantern,"
or "Jack O'Lantern."

Today, you call your Halloween pumpkin
a jack-o'-lantern.

Guy Fawkes Day

Some children in England don't celebrate Halloween. But a few days later they have fun on Guy Fawkes Day, the 5th of November.

Guy Fawkes lived a long time ago Once, he tried to blow up a building where the king was supposed to be. But he got caught.

On Guy Fawkes Day, children build a big bonfire. They also make a stuffed dummy of Guy Fawkes. To make his head, they sometimes hollow out a big turnip and carve a face on it. They stick firecrackers in the mouth and ears.

When it's night, they light the bonfire. And they shout and cheer and shoot firecrackers.

Then they lift up the dummy of Guy Fawkes. They swing him back, give him a toss, and Guy Fawkes flies into the fire! When the roaring flames reach him, the firecrackers in his mouth, go BANG! . . . BANG! . . . BANG!

Where The Word "Guy" Comes From

Do you ever call anyone a guy? Do you know why? The word comes from the name Guy Fawkes.

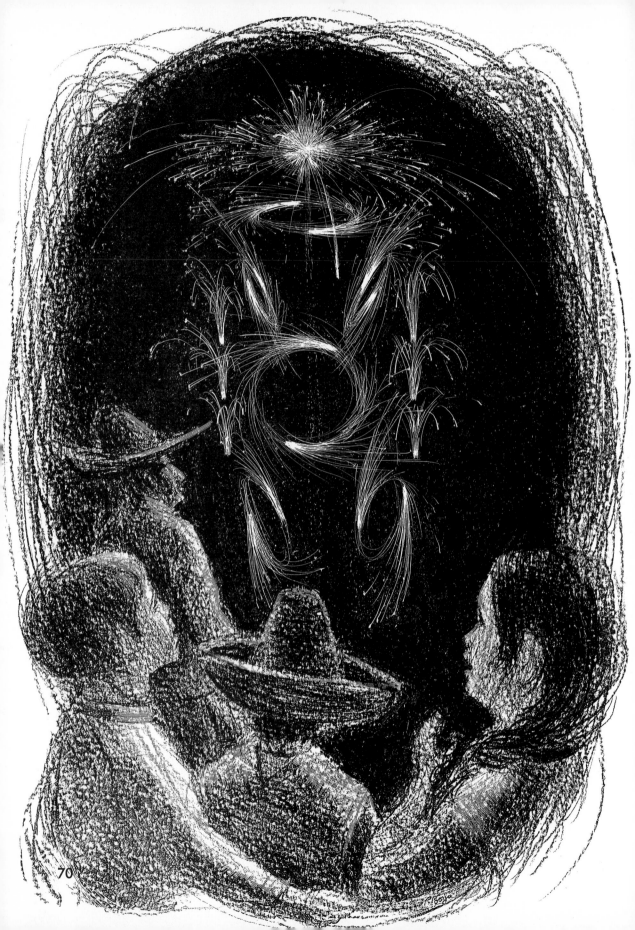

A Burning Castle...

Bam! The top of the castle blows up. Flashing lights and sparks fly everywhere.

A band plays and then, bam! Another part of the castle blows up. Piece by piece, the castle blows up and burns down until it is all gone.

But, the castle isn't a real castle. It's a make-believe castle made of wood and fireworks.

That's what you see in Mexico on Castillo day. Every town has a different Castillo day to honor its patron saint.

and a Burning House

It may seem funny to build a house and then burn it down. But in China it isn't funny. There, you build a beautiful paper house just so you can burn it down to show honor for relatives who have died.

MEN
OF
PAPER

What a funny looking man!
No wonder.
He's not really a man at all.
He's just made out of paper.

At Mardi Gras time in France,
people make the paper man
and call it King Carnival.
They sing and shout
as they carry King Carnival
through the streets.
Then they burn King Carnival
at the stake to show
that carnival time is over.

In Mexico, you can see
another funny-looking man
on the Saturday before Easter.
This one is made out of paper, too.
It hangs from a rope
in the middle of the street
and is covered
with firecrackers and presents.
When the firecrackers explode,
the paper man burns,
and the presents fall down.
The children all run
and try to catch a present.

Jump

In many places in the world,
people build bonfires just so that
they can jump over the embers
when the fire dies down.

In Belgium, an old superstition
says that if you jump over the embers
on Saint John's Eve, June 23,
you won't have stomach-aches.
But in Norway and France,
another superstition says
that if you jump over the embers,
your crops will grow
as high as you jump.

On Christmas Eve in Syria,
you might stand around a bonfire
and listen to a story with your family.
Then, when the fire dies down,
everyone jumps over the embers
and makes a wish.

Flames at Games

The games are about to begin. Suddenly, a man with a flaming torch runs onto the track. He dashes to a big bowl and dips the torch into it. The bowl bursts into flame and the crowd cheers. The Olympic Games have begun.

The Olympic Games are held every four years. And each time, before the games can start, the torch has to be brought many miles from a country called Greece, where the first of the games were held long ago.

You can see flames before other games begin, too. Sometimes football fans gather around a huge bonfire to cheer for their team. Cheerleaders jump and shout. The bonfire helps to get everyone excited and cheering.

THE YULE LOG

On the day before Christmas, men in many parts of Europe go to the woods to look for a log to burn. When they find the right one, they drag it home. The log is the Yule log.

Some people burn a Yule log for good luck. They believe they will have even more good luck if they keep it burning for the twelve days of Christmas.

They try to save a piece of the Yule log to start next year's fire. That's a sign of good luck, too!

FIREWORKS!

Red! Blue! Green! Colors shoot everywhere! There goes another sky rocket! You can see sky rockets, pinwheels, Roman candles, and many other fireworks on the Fourth of July in the United States. In some places people have fireworks displays that spell words or even make a picture.

In Italy on the Saturday before Easter, you can watch a firecracker that looks like a dove. It zooms along a wire that leads from inside a church to a cart of fireworks outside. The dove lights up the fireworks, then zooms back along the wire. Will the dove make it back to the church altar before the fireworks explode? If it does, people say they will have good luck.

If you are Chinese, you shoot firecrackers for the Chinese New Year, which usually starts in February. You might shoot fireworks to chase away evil spirits, or perhaps to honor your great, great-grandfathers.

In many other countries people also shoot off colorful fireworks displays on special days.

The Old Year Burns Out

Some of the dancers are just throwing another barrel of tar on the big bonfire. The band plays as the flames leap higher and higher. The dancers dance around and around the fire until the fire dies out.

That's the fiery way they say, "Goodbye, old year! Happy New Year!" in a little village in England. It is such an old custom that people don't even know how it began.

GIVING
AND
GETTING
GIFTS

Did you know
—that three kings
leave presents in a shoe?
—that bunnies and bells
bring Easter eggs?
—that some gifts
are hidden under pillows?

Here you can find out about
these and other ways
that people give and get gifts
on special days.

CHRISTMAS WITH STOCKINGS, SHOES, AND JARS

At Christmas,
would you like
to get your presents
in a stocking,
in a shoe,
or in a jar?

Would you like to get
your Christmas presents
from Santa Claus,
or Father Christmas,
or Saint Nicholas,
or The Three Kings,
or a Fairy Queen?

On the night before Christmas in England,
Father Christmas slips into the house
and fills your stocking with treats.
In the United States, Santa Claus is the name
of the one who fills it.

In Holland, you fill your shoes with hay and sugar
on the night before Saint Nicholas Day—
almost three weeks before Christmas.
The hay and sugar are for the horse
that Saint Nicholas rides.
After the horse eats,
Saint Nicholas fills your shoes with candy.

In Spain, you put straw in your shoes.
The straw is for the camels of The Three Kings,
who pass by and leave gifts on Epiphany,
twelve nights after Christmas.

In France, you put empty shoes on the doorstep
or by the fireplace on Christmas Eve.
The Christ Child is said to put gifts in them.

If you are in Italy, you get gifts
in a large jar, called the Urn of Fate.
It is said that a fairy queen
comes down the chimney
and fills the jar with gifts and goodies—
not on Christmas, though, but on Epiphany.

WHO BRINGS

CHRISTMAS GIFTS?

Would you be afraid if you saw
your front door suddenly fly open at night?

At Christmas time in Sweden you aren't afraid.
You know that a gift has been thrown into your house.
Grownups in Sweden tell you that an old man and woman
threw it in, and no one knows who they are.

At Christmas in some parts of Germany,
you get gifts from a girl called Christkind.
She wears a crown of candles
and carries a basket of gifts
to the children in Germany.
A terrible demon by the name of Hans Trapp
goes with Christkind.
And before Christkind gives any gifts,
Hans Trapp waves a stick
and threatens the children
who have been naughty.
In still other parts of Europe at Christmas time,
you might get a gift
from a fierce-looking man with a blackened face.
The man who gives you the gift
is called Knight Rupprecht.
With him is Saint Nicholas.

87

BE MY VALENTINE

Cards Instead of Presents

Did you ever get a card
with a picture of a heart on it?

You may have if you were
in the United States on February 14.
That day is Saint Valentine's Day.
Every year you can send
cards called valentines
to your friends and relatives.
Some of the valentines
have funny pictures and words on them.
But most of them say,
Be My Valentine.

Valentine's Day was named after
Saint Valentine, a man who
lived a long time ago.

Christmas time is another time that
you get cards and send cards.
Sending cards is one way of
wishing people
Merry Christmas, Happy New Year,
and *Happy Holidays.*

89

DAYS FOR MOTHER AND FATHER

It is two Sundays
before Christmas in Yugoslavia.
Your mother is sitting
in her chair by the window.
You quietly slip up
and tie her feet to the chair.
You shout, "Mother's Day, Mother's Day,
what will you pay to get away?"
Then your mother gives a gift to you.
As soon as you have received the gift,
you untie your mother.
The next Sunday is Father's Day,
and you do the same thing to your father.

There is a Mother's Day in May
and a Father's Day in June
in the United States.
On these days children give gifts
to their mothers and fathers.
Some children make
their parents' gifts themselves.

On Mothering Sunday in England,
about three weeks before Easter,
children give gifts to their mothers,
and small churches give gifts and flowers
to their mother churches.

Easter Bunnies and Easter Bells

Most bunnies just hop.
But the Easter bunny hops
to bring Easter eggs for you.
Sometimes the Easter bunny
puts the eggs into baskets.
Sometimes it hides the eggs
in the house,
or in the grass,
or in the garden.
Then you have to try
to find the Easter eggs.

The Easter bunny
does not take Easter eggs
to every country, though.
In France, you get your Easter eggs
from bells, instead.
There, people say
that the church bells
fly away to Italy before Easter.
When the bells fly back,
they drop eggs for you to find.

93

gifts
under
your
pillow

The Tooth Fairy
Late at night, when you are sound asleep,
a mysterious person may visit you
and put some money under your pillow.
But first you have to . . . lose a tooth!
Some people in the United States
say that if a tooth falls out
and if you put it under your pillow
when you go to bed,
the Tooth Fairy will come to take the tooth
and leave some money for you.

A Little Red Envelope
If you are in China
during the Chinese New Year's Day celebration,
you don't have to lose a tooth
to get money under your pillow.
Instead, all you do is go to sleep.
Then your mother and father put some money
in a little red envelope
and slip it under your pillow.
They put the money in an envelope that is red
because red is supposed to mean good luck.

95

Wedding Anniversaries

Can you tell how long your parents
have been married, if they get
wool gloves, wool sweaters, wool scarfs,
and a wool blanket on their wedding anniversary?

If you know about an old custom,
you'll know that gifts of wool on a wedding anniversary
mean "married seven years."

In the United States, many people give gifts
made of a certain material
to a man and woman who have been married
a certain number of years.
The anniversary is often called by the name
of the material the gifts are made of—
such as "paper anniversary" or "silver anniversary."
Here are the kinds of gifts given
for some of the anniversaries.

FIRST ANNIVERSARY
PAPER

SECOND ANNIVERSARY
COTTON OR STRAW

THIRD ANNIVERSARY
LEATHER

FOURTH ANNIVERSARY
FRUIT, FLOWERS, OR BOOKS

FIFTH ANNIVERSARY
WOOD

SIXTH ANNIVERSARY
CANDY

SEVENTH ANNIVERSARY
WOOL

EIGHTH ANNIVERSARY
POTTERY OR BRONZE

NINTH ANNIVERSARY
WILLOW OR STRAW

TENTH ANNIVERSARY
TIN

The anniversaries that mark
each twenty-five years of marriage
are usually the biggest celebrations of all

TWENTY-FIFTH ANNIVERSARY
SILVER

FIFTIETH ANNIVERSARY
GOLD

SEVENTY-FIFTH ANNIVERSARY
DIAMOND

But people don't always follow the old custom
of giving a certain kind of gift for a certain year.
They may give any gift they want to,
or send an anniversary card.

The Birthday Hat

Hurry! Don't forget the red hat. You're going to a birthday party in Japan.

The red hat is the one present that you give to your grandfather, your uncle, or your cousin when he is sixty-one years old. This is a special birthday, and the red hat is a special way of saying, "Happy birthday and many more to come."

TRICKS AND GAMES
FOR SPECIAL DAYS

Would you like
to fly a dragon kite,
play a game with Easter eggs,
ride a horse and carry a spear,
or climb a pole
all covered with grease?

These are only a few of the things
you might do on special days
in some parts of the world.
The next pages will tell you
about these and other tricks and games.

KITE FIGHTING

Have you ever had a kite fight?

You can have fun
by flying fighting kites
if you are in Thailand during the spring.

One kind of kite you can fly
is called a chula.
A chula is fast and powerful.
It is shaped like a star.

Another kind of kite is a pakpao.
It looks like a large diamond.
It can climb fast and turn sharply.

The chula kite has hooks on its string.
The pakpao kite has loops
of string hanging from it.

Pretend you are on the chula kite team.

Careful now.
Look out for the loops on the pakpao kite.
To win, you have to catch the pakpao kite
with your string of hooks.
There!
You did it!
You win the kite fight!

101

Would you like to see a flying dragon?

You can if you are in China
at the Festival of Double Nine.
On the ninth day of the ninth Chinese month
you celebrate the return of winter
by flying a kite.

Flying Dragons

The largest kite you can fly
is shaped like a dragon.
It is so big
that you need other people to help you.
First you must make sure
that you have a strong rope
fastened to your dragon.
Then you and the others
carry the dragon to a mountaintop,
where the wind will help to lift the kite
high into the sky.

Some of the other kites
you see at the festival
are shaped like fish, birds, frogs,
stars, and butterflies.
Some of the kites have holes in them
so that the wind
will make a whistling noise
when it blows through them.
The people say that by flying a kite
you will help keep away evil spirits.

103

the piñata

Your mother would be angry
if you broke a candy jar
to get a piece of candy.

But in Mexico at Christmas
you're *supposed* to break
a jar called a piñata
if you want some candy.

A piñata is a brightly colored jar
or a papier-mâché figure
that is filled with candy and gifts.
It hangs by a rope from the ceiling.

When it is your turn
to try to break the piñata,
a grownup ties a handkerchief
over your eyes so you can't peek.
Someone hands you a big stick
and turns you around and around
so that you will forget
where the piñata is.

You must try to break the piñata
by hitting it with your stick.
You keep swinging your stick
until . . . crash!
The piñata is broken!
Now you and the others
rush to get the candy and gifts.

Times When You Smash Eggs

Did you ever smash an egg on someone's head?

You can if you live in Mexico. And no one will be angry. Children there, every year a week before Lent, have a battle with eggs. The eggs are painted with bright colors and are filled with tiny pieces of colored paper. The boys form one line while the girls form another. Then the boys and the girls start to walk. As they pass one another, the boys and girls break their eggs on each other's head.

You can break eggs at Easter time in Holland, too —but not on anyone's head. Instead, you carry a basket full of hard-boiled eggs that are green, red, or yellow. Then you and the other children stand side by side in a line. You take an egg from your basket, and whoever is standing next to you takes an egg of the same color from his basket. Then you try to break his egg with yours. If you can break it before he can break yours, you get to keep both eggs. And if you get more eggs than anyone else, you win the game. In many other countries of Europe, too, you play the same kind of game.

CAT-KING

Would you like to break a barrel with a spear while riding a fast horse?

That's what you do the week before Ash Wednesday, during the spring, if you live in countries like Norway, Sweden, and Denmark.

First, some grownups hang a wooden barrel over the road. Inside the barrel is a toy cat. You are supposed to break the barrel with your spear and let the cat out. Some people believe that the cat is a sign of darkness which must be set free so that spring may come.

Giddyap! Down the road you go.

Crash! If you break the barrel and let the cat out, you are called the Cat-King.

RING ON A STRING

In autumn in the United States, you get a chance to ride on a horse and carry a spear again.

This time you are at the Buckwheat Festival in West Virginia. First, the grownups hang a ring on a string that is tied to a pole. You get on your horse and race toward the ring. Then you try to get the ring onto the end of your spear. If you do, you win.

TREATS OR ELSE

TRICK OR TREAT!

TRICK OR TREAT!

This is what you say on Halloween in the United States. You wear a costume and go from house to house asking for treats. The treats may be candy, fruit, or money. When someone gives you a treat, you must promise not to play a trick.

Holy Innocents' Day in Belgium means fun, sweets, toys, and money for you. Early on the morning of December 28, you get keys to all the rooms and closets. Then, when a grownup walks into a closet or room, you quickly lock the door. The grownup who is locked in the room or closet is called either a "sugar aunt" or a "sugar uncle." But there is one way for the sugar aunt or uncle to get out—he must promise to give you a gift.

If you live in Denmark, on the day before Ash Wednesday you tie colored paper to birch branches. Then you call them Lenten birches. You use the Lenten birches to hit either your mother or father—lightly, of course. Then they will give you some hot cross buns.

Or how would you like to be a pace egger? You can be if you go from house to house at Easter time in England. You try to get some eggs by singing a little song:

Please, Mrs. Whiteleg,
Please to give us an Easter egg.
If you won't give us an Easter egg,
Your hens will all lay addled eggs
And your cocks all lay stones.

111

APRIL FOOLS' DAY

There is a fly on the end of your nose!

Did you look to see?

If you did,
and if today is April Fools' Day,
someone may call you—
an April gowk . . . an April fish,
an April fool . . . or a noddie.
In England, you can play April Fools' Day tricks
only in the morning.
If a trick is played on you,
you are called a noddie.

In the United States, you are an April fool.

In Scotland you are an April gowk.
A gowk is another name for a cuckoo bird.

In Portugal, you celebrate two All Fools' Days—
on both the Sunday and Monday before Lent.
And the trick you play
is to throw flour at your friends.

Some people believe that
April Fools' Day began in France.

A long time ago, New Year's Day
was on April first.
Later when people decided to use a new calendar,
New Year's Day came on January first.
But some people forgot.
They celebrated at the old time.
So they were called April fools.
Today in France,
a person who has had a trick played on him
is called an April fish.

Fun on the Water

Hurry!
The dragon boat festival is about to begin.
And you are in a boat race
on an island called Taiwan.

The boat that you are going to ride in
is shaped and painted like a dragon.
Get ready with your oar.

Go!
As you row down the river,
people on the shore shout
and play trumpets, drums, and gongs.
If your boat finishes ahead of the others,
you're the winner!
Every year the people of Taiwan
have this boat race
to celebrate the coming of summer.

In another part of the world,
you can have fun on the water again.
In July at the Timber Carnival
in Albany, Oregon,
one of the games you play is called jousting.

You and the others step onto logs
that are tied together
in the shape of a square.
Then you each take a long pole
that has a ball of cloth
tied onto the end.
You run back and forth
along the log with your pole
and try to knock the other people
into the water.
If you do, you win.
If you don't, you get all wet.

115

Pancake Day

When some women make pancakes,
they don't just stay in the kitchen.
They go outside, run in a race,
and flip their pancakes while they run!

The women line up in the village square.
Each one carries a frying pan
with a hot pancake in it.
The women have to flip their pancakes
at least three times
before they reach the church door
at the other end of the square.

They're off!
Pancakes are flipping
and feet are flying.
That woman in the blue dress
is almost to the church.
Just one more flip of the pancake and . . .
she did it. She won!
Now that she has won,
she gets kissed by the church-bell ringer.

But what about the hot pancake?
The bell ringer eats it,
but if you ask him,
maybe he will give you a bite of it.

This race is held every year
on Shrove Tuesday in Olney, England.
On the same day
women in Liberal, Kansas,
also have a pancake race.

A Slippery Pole

What could be easier than sliding down a slippery pole with grease all over it? And what could be harder than trying to shinny up that same slippery pole? But that is what you try to do if you live in Palermo, Sicily, and celebrate the festival of Santa Rosalia in July.

Around the top of the pole are flowers and streamers. And at the very top are good things to eat. As you try to climb the pole, you slip and slide. So you stand on a friend's shoulders to help you reach the top. And when you reach the top, you get to keep the food that you find.

GAMES THE WORLD OVER

Do you know how
to play Tsoo Tsoo,
Lame Chicken,
or Scorpion's Sting?

Here you can read
how boys and girls
play these and other games.
You can play them, too.

bowl a ball

When you play a game called bowling,
you try to knock down ten wooden pins
by rolling a ball toward them.

But when you play a bowling game
called Nsikwi in Africa,
you roll a ball at corncobs.
Boys and girls try to knock down
each other's corncobs.
It isn't as easy as it sounds,
for sometimes the ground is bumpy.

In a ball-rolling game
that American Indians play,
you don't knock anything down.
Instead, you try to roll a ball
across a buffalo robe.
But to roll the ball, you
hit it with a stick.

DON'T PEEK!

It's no fair peeking
when you play
Blindman's Buff, no matter where
you are in the world.

When you play
Blindman's Buff in Africa,
you play with two "blind" men.
One blindfolded person
is "It," and the other
blindfolded person
clicks two sticks together.
The one who is "It"
listens carefully to find
where the clicking and clacking
is coming from.
When he does find out,
he tries to tag
the person who
is clicking the sticks.

You can also play
a blindfold game in China.
It is called Tsoo Tsoo.
The one who is "It" wears a blindfold
and is called the hen.
The other children
are called the chickens.
The "chickens" try to touch
the "hen" without getting "pecked."

In South America,
a blindfold game is played
with "hens" and "chickens."
It is called Blind Hen.

around and

around

"Ring-Around-a-Rosy"
is just one of the games
that you play in a circle.

"Wolf, wolf, are you ready?"
That is what children
in Peru shout at you
when you play Wolf.
The children stand
in a circle
around you
and keep asking
if you are ready.
You keep telling them "no"
until they get very close.
Suddenly you shout,
"Yes, I am ready!"
You chase after them
until you tag one of them.
The one you tag
is the wolf in the next game.

In Africa, you can play
Cat and Mouse in a circle.
The one who is the mouse
stands inside the circle.
The one who is the cat
stands outside the circle.
Everyone else is part of the circle.
When the circle starts moving,
the cat chases the mouse
in and out and around the circle
until he catches him.

125

ready for

One for the money!
Two for the show!
Three to get ready,
and four to GO!

Now you hop, hop, hop
in your bag to the finish line.

In many countries,
like the United States and Holland,
you can have a bag race.
You have to stand in the bag
and hold the sides up
with your hands while you
try to hop faster
than anyone else.

Or you can kick a stick
when you run a race
that Indians in America run.

Another time you use sticks
is when you run
the Lame Chicken race in China.
In that race
you put ten sticks
on the ground
so that they look
like a long ladder.
Then you hop over each stick
without touching any of them.

a race?

YOU ARE "IT"!

When you are "It"
in the United States,
you can be a spry fox
and go darting after geese.
When you are "It" in Africa,
you can be a roaring lion
and go bounding after deer.
Or you can be a ferocious wildcat
and go chasing after chickens.

When you are "It" in Denmark,
you can be a lumbering bear.

In Mexico when you are "It,"
you can be a howling wolf
and run after woolly lambs.

In all these tag games
you tag someone to make him "It."

In India, the game is harder.
It is called Scorpion's Sting.
If you are "It,"
you are the scorpion.
You walk on your hands
and one foot.
You have to keep the other foot
sticking in the air.
It is your stinger,
and you try to tag
the other players with it.

jumping rope

Jump over the rope as it
whirls around.
Everyone sings while you jump.

Teddy bear, Teddy bear
turn around.
Teddy bear, Teddy bear
touch the ground.
Teddy bear, Teddy bear
show your shoe.
Teddy bear, Teddy bear
better skiddoo.

That's a rhyme you would sing
in the United States, England, and Canada.

Another one you would sing in the United States is

Jelly in the bowl,
Jelly in the bowl,
Wiggy waggy, wiggy waggy,
Jelly in the bowl.

Still another might be

Mabel, Mabel,
set the table.
Don't forget
the salt,
vinegar,
mustard,
pepper.

And when you sing "pepper,"
you have to jump as fast as you can,
or you'll miss and be out.

Almost everywhere in the world
children jump rope.

Fun on a String

Down and up and down and Around the World. Then down and Walk the Dog. These are tricks you can do when you pull on the string of a yo-yo.

Almost wherever you go in the world you see children playing with things on strings. In Mexico, children play with a balero. A balero is made of a cup, a stick, a ball, and a string. To win the game, you have to flip the ball up into the cup.

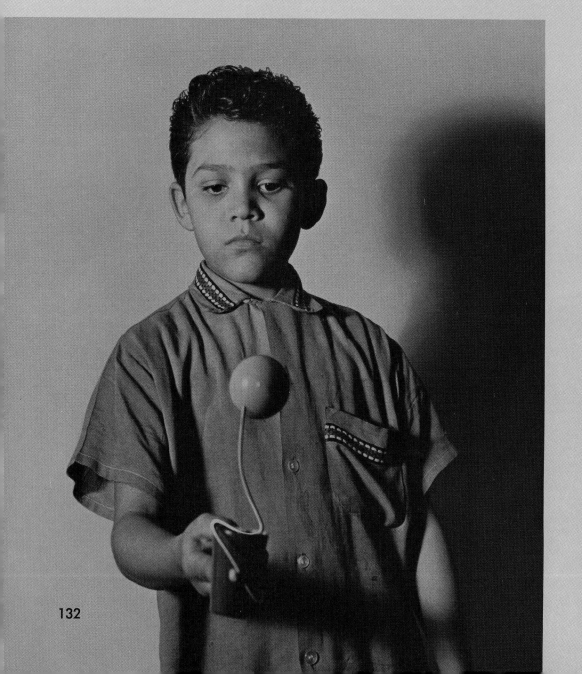

TOYS
WHEREVER
YOU GO

No matter where
in the world you go,
children play with toys.
And some of the toys
they play with
are the same as the ones
you play with.
Their balls may bounce differently,
but they are balls just the same.
Their dolls may look different,
but they still are dolls for play.
Their music boxes
may play different songs,
but still they are fun to hear.

What are the toys of the world?
Read on and see.

dolls everywhere

Everywhere in the world
children like to play
with dolls.

They might play with china dolls,
or cloth dolls,
or paper dolls,
or plastic dolls,
or rag dolls,
or stick dolls,
but still, they like
to play with dolls.

Girls in Japan
even have a special day for dolls.
On the third day of March
they put their favorite dolls
on shelves for everyone to see.

Play Ball!

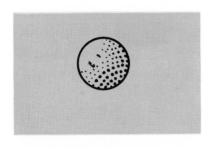

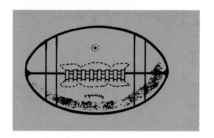

You can walk across the land
and you can sail across the seas,
but whichever way you go
you will see children
playing with balls.

They may be catching them
or throwing them.
They may be hitting them
or kicking them.
They may be spinning them
or bouncing them.
They almost always roll them.

They play ping-pong,
golf, and handball
with balls as small as a plum.

They play tennis,
cricket, and baseball
with balls the size of an orange.

They play basketball,
soccer, and volleyball
with balls as big as a pumpkin.

They even play with a ball
that looks more like
an egg than a ball.
It is a football.

music boxes

Most boxes just sit
and don't make a sound.
But some boxes play music
when you open them.
They are called
music boxes.

Music boxes can be
short or tall,
large or small.
Some look like clocks,
or like animals,
or like powder boxes,
or like little houses.
They play sad tunes
or happy tunes.

On some music boxes,
little doll people dance
and twirl around
while the music is playing.

You can go to almost
any part of the world
and hear music boxes.

139

toys
that
go
places

140

With some of your toys you can pretend to go anywhere. Dash to a fire in your fire truck. Zoom into a tunnel in your electric train. Race over the water in your speedboat. Speed around a track in your race car. Fly across the country in your airplane. Whoosh to the moon in your spaceship.

Children play with toys like these in many countries. But their toy trucks, trains, boats, cars, and airplanes may look different in other lands. They may look different because the *real* trucks, trains, boats, cars, and airplanes often look different.

houses,
forts,
and
castles

Boys and girls everywhere
build toy houses,
castles, and forts.
They build them with blocks,
cardboard, sticks,
stones, and even sand.

When they want to build
something bigger so that
they can play inside it,
sometimes they build
a house in a tree,
a fort out of snow,
or a tepee out of a blanket.

Punch and Judy

SOCK! WHAM! WHACK!

These are some of the sounds you hear when you watch a Punch-and-Judy show.

Punch and his wife Judy are funny little puppets who have huge noses, big goggling eyes, and wide, wide mouths.

Punch always stirs up trouble, and Judy gets very angry with him. They hit one another with big sticks, and they squawk loudly at each other. Punch and Judy act out their fights on a stage of their own, just like the one you see on this page.

Children in Italy saw puppet shows like Punch and Judy a long time ago. Soon children in France and England wanted to see the same kind of puppet shows. People in England named the puppets Punch and Judy.

Today, children in many lands can see a Punch-and-Judy show.

144

FOOD
FOR
SPECIAL
DAYS

Did you ever eat
a Lazybones cake,
a chocolate log,
a Cake of the Kings,
or a pudding with a button in it?

You might on special days
in some parts of the world.
On the next pages
you can find out where.

Follow the Orange Scrambler

Hooray for the orange scrambler! Without his help, the tuttimen couldn't trade an orange for a penny or a kiss.

If you visit the little town of Hungerford, England, on the Tuesday after Easter, you can see an orange scrambler and two tuttimen in a celebration.

The day is called Hock Tuesday.

Each tuttiman carries a tuttipole that is decorated with ribbons and topped with flowers and an orange. The tuttimen visit every home in the town. The orange scrambler goes with them. You and other boys and girls follow him.

At every home the tuttimen ask for pennies from the men and kisses from the women. The tuttimen give them the oranges from the tops of their tuttipoles as gifts. The orange scrambler keeps busy putting more oranges on the tops of the tuttimen's poles.

After he and the tuttimen visit the last home, the orange scrambler throws the last of his oranges to you and the other children. You run, you jump, and you scramble about to see if you can gather the most oranges.

147

Lazybones Day

Are you a lazybones?
If you are,
you have to treat your friends
to candy or cake on Lazybones Day.

In Holland, that is the day
for Lazybones cakes.
Lazybones cakes are hot cakes
with sirup on top.

Early in the morning
you and your friends
march through the streets
and make as much noise as you can.
You shout, you whistle,
and you bang on pots and pans.
When you ring a doorbell
and find a boy or girl asleep,
you shout,
Lazybones, lazybones,
tucked in his bed!
And for being a sleepyhead,
poor lazybones has to pay you
with candy or cake.

When everyone is awake,
you go to the market place.
You eat gingerbread, ice cream,
and Lazybones cakes.

Lazybones Day started long ago
because of a man named Piet Lak.
Piet Lak was a watchman
who fell asleep while enemies
marched into Holland.
After that, the people
called him Lazy Lak.
Now children remember Lazy Lak
by making as much hullabaloo
as they can early in the morning
on Lazybones Day,
about seven weeks after Easter.

Eating at Easter

At Easter time
in the United States,
you may eat
Easter eggs,
chocolate bunnies,
and chocolate lambs.

But in Poland you may eat
a special Easter cake
that is wide and looks like
an old woman's skirts.
The cake is called babka,
because "babka"
means old woman.

In Italy on the night
before Easter you eat
a special Easter pizza
made with eggs.

And in many countries
Easter is a day
for eating lamb
for dinner.

151

The Things You

Find in Pudding!

Did you ever eat pudding
and find a button or a ring in it?

You might if you live in England.
At Christmas time you eat plum pudding.
Inside the pudding are little surprises.

People say that if you find a ring,
you will be the first one married.
If you find a thimble,
you'll be an old maid.
If you find a button,
you'll be a bachelor.
And if you find a sixpence,
you'll be rich some day.

Which prize would you like
to find in your pudding?

Bobbie Burns' Birthday

Did you ever eat a pudding that was cooked in a sheep's stomach? You might if you are in Scotland.

The pudding is called haggis. You eat it on January 25 when you celebrate the birthday of a famous Scottish poet named Robert Burns, often called "Bobbie Burns."

When it is time to eat the haggis, men playing bagpipes march into the dining room from the kitchen. Behind them, a man wearing kilts and a long plaid scarf carries the haggis. Everybody cheers when they see the famous pudding.

Bobbie Burns liked the pudding so much that he called it "great chieftain o' the puddin' race."

Another special day for eating haggis is Saint Andrew's Day, on November 30. Saint Andrew is the patron saint of Scotland.

155

Cake
of
the
Kings

Whoever finds the bean in the cake is the king or the queen of the party!

If you live in France, you may have a party on January 6. You and your friends eat a Cake of the Kings. Inside the cake is one bean. If you find it in your slice of cake, your family and friends put a paper crown on your head. Then you are the ruler of the party. Everyone must do what you do. It's just like the game Follow the Leader.

The cake is called Cake of the Kings in honor of the Three Kings who visited the Christ Child long ago.

People in other countries eat a Cake of the Kings, too. People in England call the cake the Twelfth Day Cake, because January 6 is twelve days after Christmas.

SAINT JOHN'S DAY CAKE

There is a place where you can have a special day and a special cake if your name is John. On Saint John's Day, June 24, your family gives you a big cake in the shape of a J. The place is Spain.

S.Fleishman

pumpkins and turkeys

Do you know why you eat turkey and pumpkin pie on Thanksgiving Day?

A long time ago, people called the Pilgrims came to America. After their first harvest, they were so thankful to have a new land and enough food to eat, that they planned a special day for giving thanks to God.

To celebrate, they had a big dinner of the food that they found in their new land.

For part of their dinner, the Pilgrim fathers killed fat, funny-looking birds that made a "gobble, gobble" noise. They were the first Thanksgiving Day turkeys.

For dessert, the Pilgrim mothers made a pudding out of pumpkins. Those puddings were the first Thanksgiving Day pumpkin "pies."

Today, you eat turkey and pumpkin pie on Thanksgiving Day just as the Pilgrims did many years ago.

Lucky Foods for the New Year

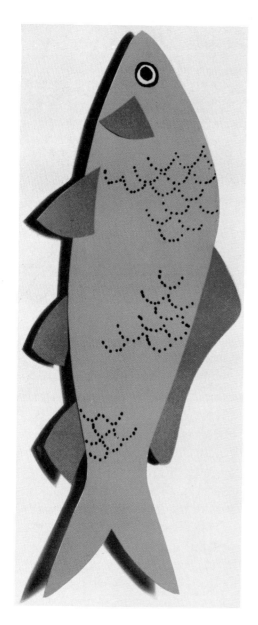

In many parts of the world,
the special food
you eat on New Year's Day
is supposed to bring you luck.

In Japan, you eat a fish called carp.
Carp are able to swim
against strong currents
and even leap waterfalls.
So, if you eat carp, people say
that you, too, will be able
to do difficult things
in the coming year.

In Hungary, if you eat a roast pig
with an apple or a four-leaf clover
in its mouth, you will have a lucky year.

In Israel, you dip apples into honey
to bring sweetness into the new year.

In other lands, you may eat
black peas to make you strong,
chestnuts to bring you success,
or even a chicken gizzard
to make you beautiful
during the coming year.

Christmas Dinner
After Midnight

Were you ever allowed to stay awake until after midnight to eat your Christmas dinner? Your parents might let you if you live in France. Almost everyone in France stays up on Christmas Eve.

Church bells ring at midnight and you and your family go to church. Then you all hurry home for midnight Christmas dinner.

After dinner you eat a special dessert—a Christmas log. But it isn't a real log. It's chocolate cake rolled up in whipped cream. Candy mushrooms and candy elves are on the top. And when you slice it, it looks something like a jelly roll.

FINGERS,
FORKS,
AND
CHOPSTICKS

Eat with your fingers,
or eat with two sticks.

Drink your soup from a bowl,
or sit on the floor when you eat.

These are good manners,
if you're in the right place.

On these pages
you can find out where.

Eating with Sticks?

If you are in China, Japan, or Hawaii, you might eat with chopsticks.

Chopsticks are two narrow sticks that are a little longer than a pencil. They are made of wood, ivory, bamboo, or plastic.

When you eat, you move one chopstick toward the other so that you can pick up your food between the sticks. Don't let the chopsticks cross. If you do, the food between the sticks will flip away.

If you practice eating with your chopsticks, soon you will be able to pick up rice, shrimp, beans, bamboo shoots, and even wet slippery noodles.

But how do you cut your meat with chopsticks? You don't have to. The meat is already cut into small pieces before it is served.

Dinner
on
the
Floor

When you eat your dinner in Japan, you sit at a table no higher than your knees. And you don't sit on a chair. You sit on the floor!

In front of you are four or five bowls, each filled with a different kind of food. Even your teacup looks like a tiny bowl because it doesn't have a handle.

But how do you eat? There are no knives, spoons, or forks.

When you have soup, you drink it out of the bowl. For the other food, you use your chopsticks.

EATING WITH FINGERS IN MALAYA

Eating with Fingers

You eat pretzels, crackers, and candy with your fingers, but do you ever eat your dinner with your fingers?

You do if you live in a country called Malaya, because people there don't use forks or chopsticks.

In Hawaii, you use your fingers to eat a pasty food called poi.

In India, you eat with your fingers, too. But to be polite, you have to be careful which hand you use. When you drink, you have to pick up your cup with your left hand. When you eat, you pick up your food with your right hand.

169

FORKS AND KNIVES

Usually, you use a knife
and a fork when you eat—
a knife to cut your food
and a fork to put the food
into your mouth.

But in the United States
it isn't always as easy as it sounds.
Some people switch knife and fork
back and forth, from hand to hand,
throughout a meal.
If you're one of these people,
after you cut a piece of food,
you put the knife on your plate.

Then you switch the fork
to your other hand
to pick up a piece of food.
The fork goes back and forth,
and the knife goes up and down
until your food is finally gone.

But some people in the United States
find that it's easier to eat the way
people in Europe and Latin America do.
They hold their forks in one hand,
and their knives in the other hand,
and hardly ever switch during a meal.
Either way is polite.

Goodies on a Stick

Sometimes you eat things that stick on sticks—taffy apples, lollipops, or ice-cream bars.

But if you visit Peru, you might eat chunks of meat that are stuck on a stick.

You buy your meat from a woman who cooks it on the street. She spears four or five chunks of meat with a stick of bamboo. Then she roasts and toasts the meat over a little stove of burning charcoal.

Just before she hands it to you, she covers the meat with a spicy sauce that stings your tongue. Then you eat it right off the stick.

IT STARTED
WITH A STORY

Where do the days of the week
and the months of the year
get their names?

Days are named after
the sun and the moon,
fierce gods of war,
and gentle goddesses.

Months are named after
gods and goddesses,
famous people, and numbers.

On the next few pages,
you can read about the stories behind
the naming of our days and months.

Sunday

Long ago, no one could explain the ball of light that traveled across the sky every day. The people who lived in southern Europe decided there must be a god who drove the ball of light across the sky. They decided to honor this god by naming a day of the week after the ball of light. They called the ball of light *sol* in their language, which was Latin. So they named the day *dies solis,* which is Latin for "day of the sun."

Later, the people who lived in northern Europe, also decided to honor the sun. But they spoke a different language. So in their language they called the day that honored the sun, *sunnandaeg,* which in English means "day of the sun." Many years later, *sunnandaeg* became *Sunday.*

A BRONZE STATUE FROM DENMARK SHOWS A
HORSE PULLING THE SUN IN A CHARIOT.

A CARVING ON A SHELL FROM ITALY
SHOWS THE ROMAN SUN GOD, APOLLO,
RIDING THROUGH THE SKY IN HIS
CHARIOT.

THE ROMAN FORUM AT NIGHT IN ROME, ITALY

Monday

The southern European people also had a name for the silver ball of light that crossed the sky at night. In Latin the name was *luna*. When they decided to name a day after *luna*, they called it *lunae dies*. Later the northern Europeans honored *mona* (that was their word for *luna*, or moon) by naming a day *monan daeg*. From *monan daeg* comes our modern English name, *Monday*.

Tuesday

People used to believe in a god of war named *Tiw*. (Some people spelled his name in different ways.) They thought that Tiw helped the warriors who worshipped him. People believed that, when a warrior died in battle, Tiw would come down from the mountain where he lived. With a group of women helpers, he would take the dead warrior to a beautiful land of rest.

To honor Tiw, they named a day of the week after him. They called this day *Tiwesdaeg*. In English it became *Tuesday*.

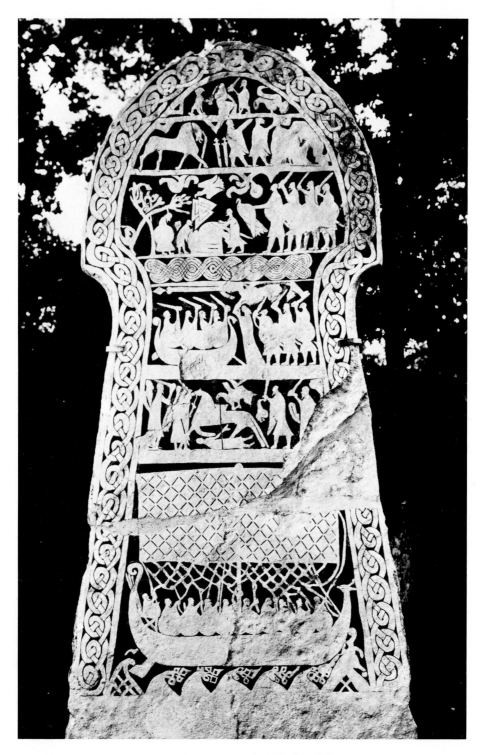

ANCIENT PICTURE STONE HONORING TIW, A GOD OF WAR

Wednesday

Certain people who used to live in northern Europe believed in many different gods. But they believed that one god was more powerful than all the others. They called this god *Woden.*

It is said that Woden wanted so much to be wise that he traveled everywhere looking for knowledge. But to get knowledge he had to give one of his eyes. After that, people say he always wore a large hat with a floppy brim that covered his missing eye.

Two black birds that acted as spies usually sat on Woden's shoulders. But at night, the birds would fly down to earth. In the morning they would return to Woden and tell him everything that they saw during the night. That's how Woden always knew everything that happened on earth.

To honor Woden, the people named a day of the week after him. They named this day *Wodnesdaeg.* In English, *Wodnesdaeg* became *Wednesday.* But it's easier to say "wensday" than to say "wed-nes-day," and that's why we pronounce it the way we do.

Thursday

Long ago, people couldn't understand what thunder and lightning were. They just saw a streak of light across the sky and they heard a loud rumbling. They decided that thunder and lightning had to be caused by a god. People in northern Europe named this god *Thor*.

They believed that when Thor was very angry, he would throw a large hammer across the sky. That was the lightning. And while he was throwing his hammer, he would ride in a wagon pulled by two goats. The sound of the wheels of the wagon was the thunder.

To honor Thor, the people who believed in him named a day of the week after him. They called this day *Thuresdaeg*. Today, in English, we say *Thursday* instead.

Friday

People used to believe in a gentle, beautiful goddess named *Frigg*. She took care of brave warriors who died on earth. One of the other gods would take a warrior to Frigg and she would bring him back to life.

The people who believed in Frigg decided to honor her by naming a day of the week after her. They called this day *Frigedaeg*. In English it became *Friday*.

FRIGG HOLDS THE SPEAR AND SHIELD IN THIS SCENE FROM RICHARD WAGNER'S OPERA, "DIE WALKÜRE."

Saturday

Long ago, in the days of the Roman Empire, people used to believe in a god of farming called *Saturn*. They believed that Saturn could make the weather good or bad, and that he had the power to control how much rain would fall.

Before a Roman farmer would plant his fields, he would try to get Saturn to give him good weather. He believed that if he killed an animal for Saturn, that would make Saturn happy. Then Saturn would make sure that the weather was good.

A MOSAIC SHOWING SCENES OF ANCIENT ROMAN FARM LIFE

Not only did the people name a planet after Saturn, but they also named a day of the week after him. They called this day *Saturni dies,* Latin words which mean "day of Saturn." In English, those words became Saturday.

THE ROMAN GOD, SATURN

THE PLANET SATURN

January

Long ago, when there were only ten months in the calendar, an emperor in Rome decided to add two more months. But he had to find names for these months.

People at that time believed in a god called *Janus,* who had two faces—one face looking into the future, and one face looking into the past. So, the emperor thought that it would be a good idea to name the first of the two new months after Janus. During this month, people could look back on what happened during the past calendar year and look forward to the new calendar year. He called this month *Januarius.* Today, in English, it is *January.*

AN OLD ROMAN COIN SHOWS THE HEADS OF JANUS.

February

Then he had to think of a name for the other new month. In those days, the calendar year started with the month we call *March*. The two new months were added at the end of the year. So this new month that the emperor had to find a name for would become the last month of the year. He decided to name the month after a Latin word that means "making clean." At that time, people often thought about the things they had done wrong during the past year, and they were sorry for them—they made themselves clean. The Latin word for "making clean" was *februum,* and the name of the month became *Februarius.* In English, it became *February.*

Julius Caesar, another emperor of Rome, later moved January and February from the end of the year to the beginning of the year. And that's where they are today.

March

Long ago, the people who lived in northern Europe named two days of the week after gods of war. They named Thursday after *Thor* and Tuesday after *Tiw*. The people who lived in southern Europe, near what we now call Rome, believed in a god of war, too. But they called him *Mars*.

The Romans wanted to honor Mars. So they named a month of the year after him. For a long time this month was called *Martius*. In English, it became *March*.

A CARVING MADE IN MARBLE
OF THE ROMAN GOD, MARS ▶

◀ A BRONZE STATUE OF MARS

THIS OLD PAINTING SHOWS FLORA, THE ROMAN GODDESS OF FLOWERS.

April

In our fourth month, the earth seems to "open up" to let plants start growing. So, the Romans of long ago named this month after a Latin word which means "to open up." The word was *aperio* and the month became *Aprilis*. In English, it became *April*.

May

The Romans used to believe in a goddess of spring and growing things. This goddess was named *Maia*. Maia protected the new plants and helped them grow. So, the Romans named a month of spring after her. They called this month *Maius*. In English, it became *May*.

June

The Romans also used to believe in a goddess named Juno. Juno was the most important goddess—the queen of goddesses. So, the Romans decided to honor her by naming another month of spring after her. They called this month *Junius*. In English, it became *June*.

July

When Julius Caesar was the ruler of Rome, one of his friends decided to honor him by naming one of the months of the year after him. He chose the month when Julius Caesar was born, and named it *Julius*. In English, it became *July*.

August

A few years later, Caesar's nephew, Augustus, took over as the ruler of Rome. Caesar Augustus wanted to be just as famous as Julius Caesar was. So, he changed the name of another month to *Augustus*. In English, it became *August*.

But Augustus went one step further. At that time, the month of July had one more day than the month of August did. So, Augustus took one day from February and added it to the month named after himself. Then the months of July and August each had 31 days. And Caesar Augustus felt he was even with Julius Caesar.

JULIUS CAESAR

CAESAR AUGUSTUS

September, October, November, December

VII

VIII

The early Roman calendar only had ten months in the year. Some of these months were named after numbers.

The Latin word for *seven* was *septem*. So the month that was once the seventh month, in the early Roman calendar became *September*. The Latin word for *eight* was *octo*. So the eighth month became *October*. The Latin word for *nine* was *novem*. So the ninth month became *November*. And the Latin word for *ten* was *decem*. So the tenth month became *December*.

IX

Later, two more months were added to the year. (If you want to read about those two months, look on pages 186 and 187 in this Volume.) Those two added months came to be the first two months of the calendar year. So, in the calendar we now use, September isn't the seventh month anymore. October isn't the eighth month anymore. November isn't the ninth month anymore, and December isn't the tenth month anymore. But we still use the old names for these months, even though they don't seem to make much sense.

X

ANIMAL
DAYS

What do animals
say at Christmas time?

What does the winner get
at a jumping frog contest?

What do children of India
do to dress up their sheep?

What do you do with a lucky pig?

What do cowboys do at rodeos?

What does the eagle stand for?

Look ahead to find the answers
to these questions
and more about holidays
and customs with animals.

"MERRY CHRISTMAS,"
Says the Horse

"Merry Christmas, Mr. Farmer," says the horse.
"Merry Christmas, Mr. Farmer," says the cow.
"Merry Christmas, Mr. Farmer," says the pig.
An old legend says
that you might hear animals talk like this
on a farm in Switzerland on the night before Christmas.
Some people there say that all the animals
can speak at midnight on Christmas Eve!
But if you were on a farm in Belgium
early on a New Year's morning,
you might hear the farmer talk like this to the animals:
"Happy New Year, Mr. Horse!"
"Happy New Year, Mrs. Cow!"
"Happy New Year, Mr. Pig!"
Some farmers there wish a Happy New Year
to all their animals.

the donkey race

Push and shove!
Yank and tug!
Make the donkeys move.
Sometimes donkeys
get stubborn,
even when they are in a race.
Then their drivers have to
ride them,
pull them,
or shove them
to the finish line.
Each driver starts out
with his donkey hitched in front
of a gaily decorated cart.
But often he ends up by
pulling the cart—and the donkey!
This donkey race is run
every February 22 on an island
called Saint Croix in the Virgin Islands.
When it is over,
the best donkey gets a prize.
But even if a donkey loses the race,
it might get a prize anyway—
it may have pulled
the best-decorated cart of all!

199

THE JUMPING FROG CONTEST

HOP—KERPLOP!
There goes the frog.
HOP—KERPLOP!
And once more,
HOP—KERPLOP!
It's a jumping frog contest!
Each frog gets only three jumps
to show that he can jump the farthest.
The frog that wins
has his name put on a silver cup!
People from many parts of the world
bring their frogs to this contest
in California every year in May.

Mark Twain wrote a story
about this contest and called it
"The Celebrated Jumping Frog
of Calaveras County."

OUR
FEATHERED
FRIENDS

School children
in the United States and Canada
have a special day
in the spring
to honor birds.
It is called Bird Day.

People honor birds in other ways, too.
The bird that wins the singing contest
in the Harz Mountains in Germany
gets his cage decorated with flowers.
People there raise canaries
and bring them together
on Pentecost Day,
fifty days after Easter,
to find out which one is the best singer.

People in Salt Lake City, Utah,
even built a tower to honor seagulls!
They did this to remember the seagulls
that ate great swarms of pesky crickets
that were ruining the plants there.

202

THE SEA GULL MONUMENT,
SALT LAKE CITY, UTAH

dress-up time for

DECORATED CATTLE IN INDIA

animals

After a horse wins a race,
race-track men sometimes
dress up the horse
with a collar of flowers.

Other animals get dressed up, too.
In India, you see cattle
covered with ornaments
and sheep spotted with paint!
At a celebration called the Bull Festival,
people decorate their cattle
and parade them through the streets.
For another special time, called Ramadan,
some of the children
dress up their pet sheep
with spots of paint.

Horses, cows, and sheep
get dressed up in Mexico, too.
On January 17,
the feast of Saint Anthony,
you can see these animals along with
dogs and cats, pigs and goats,
and even chickens, turkeys,
and other birds,
all cleaned and dressed
with flowers and ribbons.
The children and grownups there
want to keep their animals healthy
and make them mind.
So they bring these decorated animals
to the village churchyard to be blessed.

A DECORATED HORSE

GOOD-LUCK animals

Some people say a rabbit's foot or the wishbone of a turkey is a sign of good luck. And others say that whole animals can bring good luck!

Imagine you are sitting in a restaurant in a city called Vienna. The people around you are happy and gay because it is almost midnight on New Year's Eve. Suddenly you hear a noise—"Oink, oink." People scramble and run. They're chasing a pig! There he goes—around waiters' legs and under tabletops! Hurry and reach! If you can touch him, you will have good luck. That's what the people of Vienna say.

Even little crickets mean good luck. In China and Japan, people keep them in bamboo cages at home.

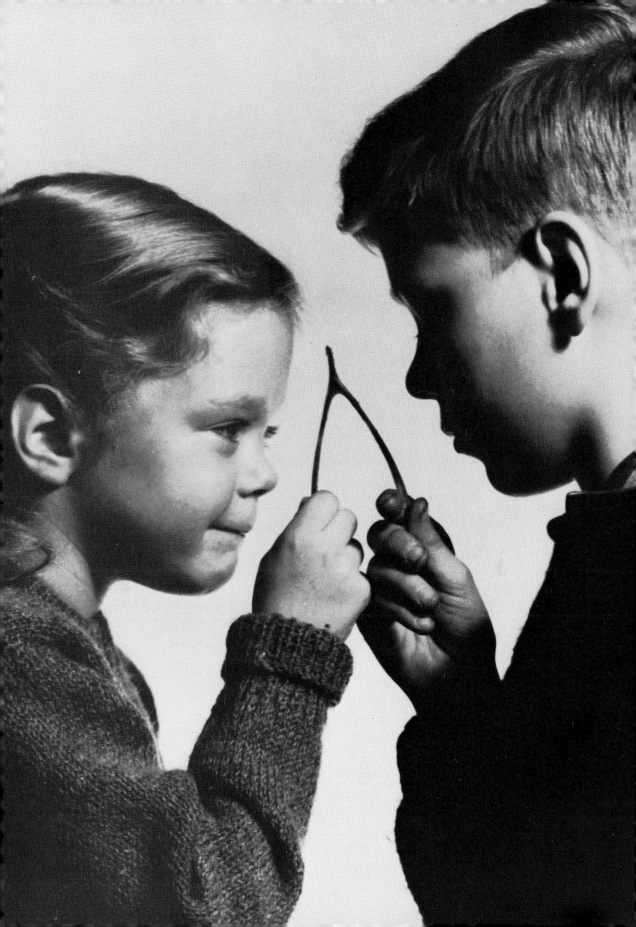

Here Come

the BULLS!

Here come the bulls!
Hurry!
Off the street!
Before the big bullfight
on San Fermín Day in July
in Pamplona, Spain,
people think it is great fun
to let angry bulls
chase them through the streets!

Later in the afternoon,
you can go along with the crowd
to watch the big bullfight.
Trumpets blare!
The crowd roars!
Here comes the bull!
And there is the man
that will fight him!
In this fight, the man must prove
that he is the master of the bull.
You can see this kind of bullfight
in other parts of Europe
and in Latin America, too.

You can watch
a different kind of bullfight
in some parts of Japan.
These bullfights
are not between a man and a bull,
but between one bull and another!

209

RODEO!

Do you want to
ride a bucking bronco,
rope a running calf,
ride or wrestle a wild bull?
Then a rodeo is for you!
You have to be a good rider or roper
to be a rodeo cowboy or cowgirl.
But if you do your job well,
you may win a prize!

Rodeos started long ago
at round-up time,
when cowboys got
all their cattle together
to count them.
When they finished their work,
the cowboys took time off to find out
who was best at riding and roping.
You can still see
famous rodeos every year
in the United States and in Canada.

Animal Mascots

The next time
you see a fire truck
zoom down the street,
see if you can spot a dog
riding with the firemen.
Firemen often have a dog
as a mascot at the firehouse.
Sometimes he even
goes to the fires!

Firemen aren't
the only people
that have favorite animals
as mascots.
At a school for soldiers,
called West Point, the students
have a mule for their mascot.
At a school for sailors,
called Annapolis,
the students have a goat.
And students
at the Air Force Academy
have a falcon for their mascot.

213

CHINESE YEARS ARE DIFFERENT

The pig goes out
and the mouse comes in.
This is how
a Chinese year can begin.
Chinese people name
each year for an animal.
It may be an animal
that is big or small,
or one that is real
or not living at all.
Twelve different animals
run, creep, crawl,
or leap their way
through the years.

The Year of the Mouse is first
in the Chinese list of years.
Then comes the Year of the Ox,
the Year of the Tiger,
the Year of the Rabbit,
the Year of the Dragon,
the Year of the Snake,
the Year of the Horse,
the Year of the Sheep,
the Year of the Monkey,
the Year of the Rooster,
the Year of the Dog,
and last on the list
is the Year of the Pig.

And when the Year of the Pig
is over and done,
it is time for
the Year of the Mouse again.

Animals and Countries

Do you have a quarter?
If you do, look for the picture
of the eagle on one side.
The picture of the eagle stands for
the United States of America.
Many years ago, the people
chose the eagle to stand for
strength, skill, and bravery.
They put its picture
on their coins and paper money.

Pictures of other animals stand for
other countries.
Other countries have favorite animals, too.
In Sweden, it is the fierce lion.
In a little country called Laos,
it is the great big elephant.
And in a country called Australia,
there are two favorites—
a bird called the emu
and a bouncy kangaroo.

Four-Footed Forecaster

Do you think that animals can tell you what the weather will be? Some people have a superstition that says that the ground hog can. The ground hog is a small furry animal that is sometimes called the woodchuck. On the second day of February, if the ground hog comes out of his home in the ground and sees his shadow, he will be frightened and crawl back into his hole. People say that this means there will be six more weeks of winter. But if he cannot see his shadow, and stays out of his hole, it means that spring weather will come soon.

SIGNS, LIGHTS, AND COLORS

Do you know what a sign
with eight sides means?
Do you know what the lights
on an airplane mean?
Here you can find out about
signs, lights, and colors
that mean something.

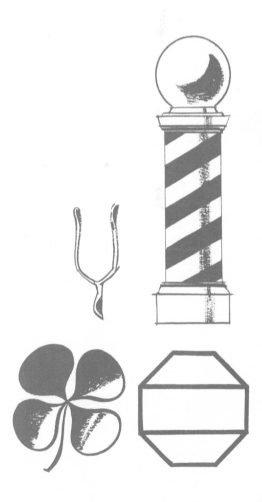

ROAD SIGNS

Cars, trucks, and buses
go up and down the streets.
They slow down.
They stop.
They go.
How do the drivers keep
from having accidents?

PARKING

One way is by knowing
what the road signs mean.

MEN WORKING

In the United States,
drivers know that a sign
with eight sides means stop.
They know that a sign
with three sides means
let the other car go first.
When drivers see a sign
with a big "X" on it, they know
that railroad tracks are ahead.
When they see a sign
with four sides, they know
that it usually means be careful.

SLIPPERY ROAD

In Europe, road signs
have pictures on them
so that no matter
what language you speak,
you can understand them.

WATCH FOR ANIMALS

BICYCLE PATH

WATCH FOR CHILDREN

TELEPHONE

WHAT PLACE IS THIS ?

Sometimes when you are looking
for a store or a shop,
signs without words
can help you find
the shop you want.

A pole that looks like
a big candy cane stands in front
of a barbershop.

There are three round balls
hanging outside of a pawnshop.
A pawnshop is a shop where
you can borrow money
by leaving something you own.

When you see a sign that looks like
a big jar with a stick in it,
you know you are looking
at a drugstore.

You can see signs without words
in many countries.
The pictures on these pages
show you some of them.

PAWNSHOP—UNITED STATES

BARBERSHOP—UNITED STATES

DRUGSTORE—SWITZERLAND

COBBLER SHOP—DENMARK

GLOVE SHOP—BELGIUM

HARDWARE SHOP—DENMARK

LOCKSMITH—SWITZERLAND

223

Beacons
and
Blinkers

If you sail a ship at night, you have to watch for the lights of other ships.

Some of the lights that you watch for are the red lights and the green lights. They can tell you which way a ship is sailing, and they help you keep from crashing.

The red light on a ship is always on her left, or port side. The green light is always on her right, or starboard side.

Airplanes also have red and green lights. There is a red light on the left wing, and a green light on the right wing.

A pilot has to know what other lights mean, too.

He can find an airport from faraway by the flashing green and white lights at the airport. Green lights show him the ends of runways. White lights show him the runways. Blue lights show him how to get to the runways for take-off.

Flag Colors

See the flag fluttering in the breeze?
It is the flag of the United States.
Sometimes it is called, "Old Glory,"
or the "Stars and Stripes."
Red, white, and blue are its colors.
And each color means something.
Red means courage—we try to be brave.
White means purity—we try to be good.
Blue means justice—we try to play fair.

The colors of other flags
mean something, too.

The flag of Norway has
red for the hearts of the people,
blue for the fields and oceans,
and white for the snow.

The flag of the Philippines has white in it, too.
The white stands for people working together.

There's one flag that is all white.
Maybe you've used it in a snowball fight
or a game of cowboys and Indians.
It's the flag that says "I give up."

a picture

228

for a country

Do you have an Uncle Sam?
Everybody in the United States
has an Uncle Sam.

He is a tall, thin man
with striped trousers and a tall hat.
He wears a vest
that is covered with stars.
You can see his picture on signs,
in newspapers, and in magazines.

But, Uncle Sam is not a real uncle.
He is a picture that stands
for the United States.

People of other countries use pictures
to stand for their countries, too.

John Bull is short and fat.
He wears his trousers
tucked into his boots,
and his vest looks like
the British flag.
John Bull is not
a real person, either.
But his picture
stands for the country
called England.

A picture of a furry bear stands
for the country sometimes called Russia
and sometimes called the Soviet Union.
Sometimes the bear has the design
of the Russian flag on it.

A picture of a dragon stands for
the country called China.
Sometimes the dragon
has a red ball.
The ball stands for the sun or moon.

WHAT'S YOUR LUCK ?

good luck!	
	HORSESHOE
bad luck!	
	BREAK A MIRROR
I wish!	
	WISHBONE

Some people say
—that if you stub your toe,
you'll have bad luck.
—that if you see a pin and pick it up,
all the day you'll have good luck.
—that if you cross your fingers
when you make a wish,
your wish will come true.
They say that 13 is an unlucky number,
and that 3 is a lucky number.
These are sayings called superstitions.
Do you know any others?

FOUR-LEAF
CLOVER

RABBIT'S FOOT

BUBBLES ON COFFEE

FIND
A PENNY

WALK UNDER
A LADDER

BLACK CAT

SPILLING SALT

STEP ON
A CRACK

FALLING STAR

CROSS A BRIDGE

WISHING WELL

BIRTHDAY
CAKE

Pictures for Ideas

Sometimes people use pictures to stand for ideas.

A picture of a woman holding a pair of scales means justice, or being fair to all. The woman in the picture is blindfolded to show that she doesn't like one side more than the other.

When people aren't fighting and when everyone is friendly, they are at peace. The picture for peace is a dove with an olive branch in its mouth.

At a theater you might see a picture of a smiling mask next to a frowning mask. The smiling mask means comedy, or something funny. The frowning mask means tragedy, or something sad.

232

WAYS
TO SAY
THINGS

Talking is easy.
You do it every day.

You talk to say
things to people.
You listen to hear
what they say to you.

No matter where
you are in the world,
you can use special words
to mean hello or good-bye,
to mean look out,
or to mean I like it.
You can use other words
to talk to animals
or to tell who you are.

But words are not all you use.
You can also talk with
your fingers,
your hands,
your shoulders,
your eyes,
and your head.

nods, winks,

and shrugs

You can say many things
without using a word.

You can nod your head to say "yes,"
shake your head to say "no,"
wink an eye to say "I'm kidding,"
and shrug your shoulders
to say "I don't know."

With a finger in front of your lips,
you can say "Shhh! Don't make a sound."

And when you make an "O" with your fingers,
you're saying "Very good."

235

When you see a friend you say hello.
When you leave a friend you say good-bye.

But in some places in the world,
people use the same word
for hello and good-bye—
in Hawaii it is "aloha,"
in Israel it is "shalom,"
and in Italy sometimes it is "ciau"
(you say it "chow").

You can also say hello and good-bye
with a handshake, a wave,
a kiss, or a hug.

HELLO and

If you live in Latin America,
you greet close friends
with a hug called an abrazo.
Your father and your mother
greet their close friends this way, too.

In Japan, people bow their heads
when they meet or say good-bye.

And if you visit Greenland,
you see Eskimos
pressing their noses together.
That is their way
of greeting each other.

GOOD-BYE

hurray!

If you dance,
sing, or act
on a stage,
how do people in the audience let you know
that they like your performance?
They clap their hands.
Sometimes they stand.
Sometimes they shout,
"Bravo" or "Hurray."
Sometimes they yell, "Encore, encore!"
This means that they like your act so much
that they want you to do it again.

How do you thank your audience?
If you're a boy, you bow.
If you're a girl, you curtsy.

INDIAN SIGN LANGUAGE

How would you talk if all your friends
spoke a different language?

Maybe you would talk by making signs
the way that American Indians used to do.

Long ago, when Indians of one tribe
met Indians of another tribe,
they had to make signs with their hands
to understand each other.

These are some of the signs they made.
Maybe you can make them, too.

When you are hungry,
you move your right hand
back and forth across your stomach.

When you mean "let's eat,"
you cup your right hand
and move it up and down
in front of your mouth.

When you have had enough to eat,
you spread your thumb
and first finger apart, and move your hand
from your chest to your chin.

If you have a tummy-ache,
you put both hands on your stomach,
and move them back and forth.

"I'M HUNGRY!" "LET'S EAT!"

"I'M FULL!" "MY STOMACH ACHES!"

241

242

"MUSH"

HOW TO TALK TO ANIMALS

Do animals understand
when you talk to them?
Sometimes they do,
but you have to know
the right words.

If you say "giddyap" to a dog,
it won't understand.
Nobody ever taught dogs
what giddyap means.
But a horse knows
that "giddyap" means "run!"
and that "whoa-o-o" means "stop."
Somebody taught the horse
what those words mean.

If you drive a mule,
you holler "gee-e-e"
to steer to the right.
You holler "haw"
to steer to the left.
Be careful not to call "gee-e-e"
when you mean "haw"
or your mule will turn
the wrong way.

If you drive a dog sled
the way the Eskimos do,
you holler, "Mush, mush"
when you want the dogs to run.

arm talk

After a pilot lands an airplane,
he has to "park" it.
To help him,
a man stands near the plane
waving his arms.
The roaring engines are so loud
that the man has to use
his arms to tell the pilot
which way to turn his plane.

Men who work in noisy factories
have to talk with their arms, too.

In a steel mill you can hear
clangs, bangs, booms, and roars.
You see a steelworker
wave his arms
to tell other workers
when to pour hot liquid iron
into a big open furnace.

Other men who talk
with their hands and arms
are traffic policemen,
men on the railroad,
men in the navy,
and men who survey
and measure land.

WATCH OUT!

Sometimes you use words
to tell people
to get out of the way,
so that they won't get hurt.

If you are a lumberjack
and chop down a giant tree,
you yell, "TIMBER-R-R-R!"
as loudly as you can
to warn people to look out
for the falling tree.

When you play golf,
you use a word
to warn people, too.
If it looks as if your ball
is going toward other players
on the golf course,
you holler, "FORE!"
This tells them
to get out of the way
so that they won't get whacked
on the head
with your golf ball.

"JIGGERS" is a word
you might use
to warn a friend
to be careful
or he'll be caught.

247

ways

Soldiers salute
when they pass each other.

248

to show respect

When a grownup comes into the room,
you jump to your feet.
And if that grownup happens to be
a king or a queen,
you curtsy if you are a girl,
or bow if you are a boy.
You do this to show your
respect for people.

You also use words to show your respect.
You say—
   "Your Majesty" to a king or a queen,
   "Your Excellency" to a bishop,
   "Your Honor" to a judge, and
   "Sir" to any man.

You can show your respect in many
other ways, too.

If you live in Japan, you bow.
Even at school you bow to your teacher.

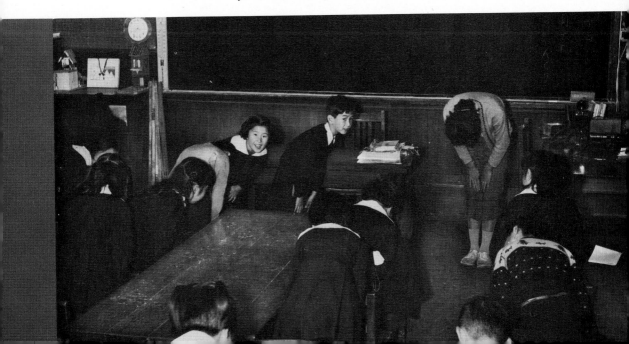

What Some Names Mean

You have a first name to tell who you are. You have a last name to tell who your family is.

But a long, long time ago, people didn't have last names. They had to invent last names because there were too many Charlies, too many Roberts, and too many Marys. People started to ask, which Charlie? Which Robert? Which Mary?

So if a Charlie was a carpenter, he became Charlie Carpenter. If a Robert was a son of Peter, he became Robert Peterson. If a Mary lived near the woods, she became Mary Woods.

This is the way that some last names started long, long ago. Do you know what your last name means?

LETTERS
AND
NUMBERS

To talk,
you use your voice.
But to write,
you use letters and numbers.
You can play with the letters
and numbers, too.
You can look
for pictures in them.
And you can look
for them in pictures.

Here's how you do it.

A

B

THE ALPHABET

Sometimes the letters in the alphabet look like pictures of things.

A
may look like a tepee with a bar across it.

B
may look like a butterfly flying sideways.

C
could be like the handle on your teacup.

A PAINTING CALLED "THE JUGGLER" BY MARC CHAGALL

JkHF
CiIeL
LjjK
EfJd
JmJGD
E Nf
H cnh G
bggdgd
GIEIDIE
kaMI
BdANij
mei

Can you find any shapes
like the shapes of these letters in the painting on the
opposite page?

A RUG CALLED "MIMOSA RUG" BY HENRI MATISSE

Can you find any shapes like the shapes of these letters in the work of art on the opposite page?

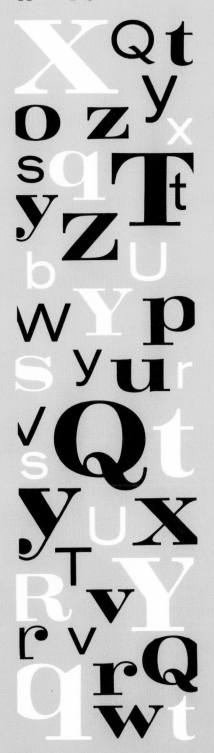

MARKS THAT TELL HOW MANY

You count things with numbers. And to write down how many things that you count, you make marks that stand for the numbers.

Numbers can look like pictures of things, too.

1

may look like a soldier standing straight and tall.

2

may look like a little girl saying her prayers.

3

may look like a bird flying on its side.

A PAINTING CALLED "HARBOR OF PORTOFINO" BY LUDWIG BEMELMANS

37410 569 8 75
97 8 7 4 4
9 64 7 10 2 786
05 95 7 942 109

Can you find any shapes like the shapes
of these numbers in the famous painting above?

SINGING
AND DANCING
AROUND
THE WORLD

In all countries,
people like to sing and dance.

They sing songs when they work.
They sing songs for holidays.
And they sing songs
to honor their country.

They dance for joy.

They dance to win wars.
They dance to imitate animals.
And they dance
to show their skill.

On these pages,
you can read about different kinds
of songs and dances.

Songs of Patriots

BATTLE OF FORT McHENRY

The special song for all people of a country is the country's national anthem. Some anthems, like the one for the people of the United States, were written during wartime.

Long ago, the United States and Great Britain had a war. In one battle, bombs and rockets shot back and forth almost all night, between the British ships in Chesapeake Bay and Fort McHenry on the American shore. When the sun came up the next morning, an American prisoner on one of the British ships saw the flag of the United States still flying over the fort. He was so glad that his country had won the battle that he wrote a song about the flag. The prisoner's name was Francis Scott Key. The song that he wrote is "The Star-Spangled Banner."

The people of France have an anthem that was written many years ago at the time of the French Revolution.

Imagine you are walking down a street in Paris, France, at that time. Suddenly, you hear the sound of marching men. French soldiers from a city called Marseille are marching to a battle. You hear them sing— "Let's go, sons of France the day of glory is here!" This song was called "The Marseillaise" (say, Mar-say-ez), and it became the French national anthem.

SONGS
TO HELP
WITH WORK

Maybe you've heard
your mother or father hum songs
as they work around the house.
Ask them why they do
and they might say that it makes
their work seem easier.

People in many parts of the world
sing songs to help them
with their work.
Long ago, when boatmen pulled
their heavy barges
along the Volga River in Russia,
they sang slow, drawn-out songs
to fit the work they did.

Yeo, heave ho! Round the capstan go.
Yeo, heave ho! Cheerily we go.
If you worked on a sailing ship
long ago, you and the other sailors
would sing a song like this
as you steadily worked
to pull up the ship's anchor.

Cowboys sing as they work at night
watching over cattle.
They sing slow, easy-moving songs
to keep the cattle quiet
and to pass the long night away.

Singing helps with heavier work, too.
Moving day in the Philippines
sometimes means lifting a whole house
and taking it to another place.
The movers often sing songs
to help them work together
with the heavy house.

Silent Night

One Christmas Eve long ago in Austria,
a church organist named Franz Gruber
was talking to Father Mohr,
the pastor of the church.
"The organ is broken, Father!
What shall we do?
If only we had a new Christmas song
that we could sing without organ music!"
Then Father Mohr decided
to write words to a new song.
When he finished,
he gave the words to Franz Gruber
so that he could write the music.
The song that he wrote was
the Christmas carol called "Silent Night."
They sang it to the soft music
of a little guitar!

DANCE AROUND A POLE

You play "ring-around-a-rosy"
by walking around in a circle
with your friends.
But a long time ago,
this game was really a dance
and instead of making
a "ring-around-a-rosy,"
grownups danced around a tree.
People in many parts of Europe
still do a circle dance.
But now they dance around a pole.
They call it the Maypole
and they decorate it
with ribbons and flowers.
They do the Maypole dance
every year on
the first day of May.

If you are a flying dancer in Mexico
you don't dance around a pole.
Instead, you fly around it.

On Corpus Christi Day,
about two months after Easter,
you and other flying dancers
climb to the top of a tall pole.
You have to be careful.
The pole is almost as tall
as five telephone poles!
Then you tie your feet with ropes
that are wound around
the top of the pole.
When you hear the music
of a drum and a flute,
you jump away from the pole
and the rope starts to unwind.
You spin around and around,
lower and lower,
faster and faster,
in wider and wider circles
until you finally reach the ground.

Fire Dances

Sparks fly from burning torches
and the fiery flames of a huge bonfire
reach up toward the sky!
It's the Navajo Indian fire dance!
Around and around the bonfire the Indians leap
almost as high as the flames themselves.
As they dance closer and closer to the fire,
you can see how their bodies are painted white
to shield them from the terrific heat.
Wherever you look, white figures leap and dance,
and sparks and flames seem to explode in the sky.

Now the flames are getting lower.
Finally, only the ashes remain.
The dance is over.

Fire dancers on the island of Sumatra
don't dance around a fire.
They carry fires with them when they dance.
They carry little lamps
that burn with a bright flame.
Each dancer holds two lamps—
one in his right hand,
and one in his left hand.
You would have to be a very careful dancer
to do a fire dance in Sumatra.

INDIAN DANCER

272

GERMAN DANCERS

JAPANESE DANCERS

Dancing Musicians

Some people dance and make music
at the same time.

Dancers in Spain make music
with wooden clappers called castanets.
The castanets fit on their fingers.
When they flutter their fingers,
the castanets clatter,
and the dancers can dance
while they play their own music.

Dancers in India would rather jingle than clatter.
They wear bells when they dance.
The bells dangle from bands
on the dancers' ankles.
Whenever the dancers stamp their feet,
the bells make a jingling sound.

Dancers in Germany don't use bells or clappers
to make music while they dance.
They just clap their hands, stamp their feet,
and click their tongues.

Dancers in Japan clap
pieces of wood together
instead of clapping their hands.
The CLICK-CLICK-CLICK of the wood
makes music for their dancing.

273

DAREDEVIL DANCES

You may think that dances are easy, but some dances are so hard that only a few people can do them. Could you do these?

Could you dance the tinikling with dancers in the Philippines? You have to move your feet quickly when you do this dance. Two people hold two bamboo poles close to the ground. They clack the poles together—CLICKETY-CLACK CLICKETY-CLACK— faster and faster as you hop in and out between the poles. You have to keep time with the clickety-clack, or the poles will catch your feet.

You may be quick enough to do that dance, but are you steady enough to do a stilt dance with dancers in Japan? You have to have good balance to dance high off the ground on tall, wooden stilts. If you aren't careful, you'll topple *down, down, down*.

If you would rather dance close to the ground, you might try a dance called the limbo. You can do the limbo with dancers in Trinidad. Two people lower a pole while you slither underneath, bending your knees and leaning far backwards. This dance is like a game. You lose if you touch the pole or if you fall.

TINIKLING DANCE

LIMBO DANCE

DANCING
WITH
SWORDS
AND
RIFLES

People may fight with swords and rifles.
But in some parts of the world,
they dance with them.

A sword dancer in Scotland
lays his sword and scabbard on the ground
in the shape of a cross.
When he dances,
he steps carefully around the cross
so that his feet never touch the sword
or the scabbard.

You'd better not get in the way
of sword dancers in Albania.
When they dance, they swish their swords
over their heads.

When men in Arabia do a rifle dance,
they dance in a circle as fast as they can.
Then they whirl around
to face the center of the circle,
point their rifles up toward the sky,
and . . . BLAM!
They all shoot their rifles at once.

Hands That Tell a Story

Twist your hands together like this to make a flying bird.

Now try to make a lotus flower with your hands like this

Then open them
to make the lotus bloom!

People in India and other parts of the world make hand pictures like these when they dance. By making pictures with their hands and moving their bodies about, they tell a story as they dance!

People in Hawaii also make hand pictures while they dance. In a dance called the hula, the dancers sometimes keep their feet almost still and move only their hands, arms, and hips. The hands go up and down and back and forth. They make one picture after another to tell a story without words.

Dance Around a Hat

A hat can be a good dancing partner. It never gets tired and it never trips.

In the Mexican hat dance, a tall hat with a wide brim sits on the floor. A man and a woman hop around it. Sometimes, the man tries to catch the woman by chasing her around the hat. But the hat keeps them apart. Finally, the woman picks up the hat and puts it on her head. Now the man can catch the woman and dance with her.

HOMES IN MANY LANDS

In some countries, if a friend said,
"Come over to my house and play!"
you might have to
climb up to a tree house,
crawl into a snow igloo,
walk into a grass hut,
or cross a bridge
to get to a houseboat.

Here you can learn about
the homes of people
from many parts
of the world.

Mud Homes

After a rainy day, you may like to go outside and slosh in the mud and make mud pies. But some people don't just play with mud. They use it to build their homes.

In the jungles of Africa, people pack mud around sticks in the shape of a hut. Then they smooth the mud with water, and let their mud huts bake in the sun. They make the roofs of the huts out of grass. If you see the huts from far away, you might think that the huts are hills, not homes. But when you see a little girl or boy running out of one of those hills, you know that you are looking at homes.

Some people in Egypt also build houses with mud. They mix mud and straw to make bricks. They put the bricks together to make thick walls that keep out the heat of the sun.

MUD HOUSES IN EGYPT

282

MUD HOUSES IN AFRICA

TENT IN AFRICA

TENT IN TIBET

Living in Tents

You could fold up your house
if your house were a tent.

Goatherds in the deserts of Africa
sometimes live in tents.
Their tents shield them
from the hot sun.
The goatherds lift up the sides
of their tents
so cool breezes can blow in.
But they quickly put down the sides
if the wind starts
to blast sand at them.
When the men move their goats
to another place,
they tie their tents around poles.
Then they can carry
their homes with them.

Have you ever heard
of a yurt or a yak?
A yurt is a kind of tent.
A yak is a kind of cow.
Some people in a land called Tibet
use yak hair to make yurts.
They cover frames of wood
with cloth made of the yak hair.
When the people want to travel,
they fold up their yurts
and carry them away.

285

HOUSES ON LEGS

Some houses have long legs. These houses stand on stilts or they sit high in trees.

Houses on stilts have many legs. You can see stilt houses on an island called Borneo. There is so much room between the floors and the ground that people can keep their cows underneath the houses. Fences between the stilts protect the cows from wild animals.

Only fish live beneath the stilt houses in some South Pacific Islands where people built homes right in the middle of a lake.

There are people in a land called Malaya who want to live even higher off the ground. So they build their houses in trees. These houses have just one leg—it is a big tree trunk.

When wild animals chase someone, he runs to his tree and scurries up the ladder. Soon the animals find nothing but tree trunks and leaves. If *you* look closely, though, you can see houses perched in those trees.

STILT HOUSE IN BORNEO

286

HOUSEBOAT IN INDIA

HOUSEBOATS IN CHINA

People who live in the kind of houses
you see in these pictures
can go on a trip while they stay at home.
They can fish in their back yards,
and they can dive out their windows.
They live in houseboats.

A houseboat in India
has big windows and a pointed roof,
just like a house on land.
But don't try to go down
to the basement
or you'll find yourself
swimming with fishes.

Houses That Float

Houseboats in China
are called sampans.
If you live on a sampan,
you can hoist up a sail
and ride your house down the river.
When your mother wants to shop,
she doesn't have to walk to the market.
The stores are on boats,
and the market can float
to your house.
Before your mother
looks at the store goods,
she ties one end of a rope around you
so that you won't fall off
with a SPLASH!

Amazing Grass Houses

You don't live in a house
that you can lift.
But some people who live in Africa
can pick up their houses
and carry them!
They make their houses from grass.
These houses look like baskets
turned upside down.
The people weave grass
to make walls and a roof.
The grass keeps the rain
from dripping down on their heads,
and it shades the people
from the hot sun.
The grass houses are so light
that maybe you and a friend
could lift one up, too.

You don't live in a house
that swells and shrinks.
But some people in Africa do.
They build grass houses that swell
when the rain pours down
and shrink when the sun shines.
People make these houses
with grass mats.
When it rains, the grass swells
until the mats become so tight
that the rain can't soak in.
But when the sun comes out,
the grass shrinks
and it makes holes in the mats
for the breezes to blow through.

A Snow House

If you are an Eskimo in Canada, you may make your house from snow.

An Eskimo house is called an igloo. Eskimos build one kind of igloo with blocks of hard-packed snow. A snow igloo looks like the back of a big, white turtle made of giant ice cubes.

You crawl into the igloo through a tunnel. It is warm inside the igloo because the freezing wind can't blow through the walls of snow or the windows of ice.

A hole at the top of the igloo lets in some air so that you can breathe. At night you put away your toys on shelves carved in the snow, and you go to sleep wrapped in furs on your bed of ice.

ORNAMENTS
AND
DECORATIONS

Here you can find out about
pictures that people make
on the ground,
pictures that people put
on their skin,
poles that people carve
out of wood,
feathers that people put
in their noses,
and many other things
that people use for decoration.

WHY PEOPLE PAINT FACES

Why do people paint their faces—
to scare others,
or to celebrate,
or to look prettier?

In Africa
and the South Sea Islands,
some people believe
that the paint
on their faces
will frighten
evil spirits away.

Long ago, Indians
in the United States
painted their faces
when they went to war.
They believed
that the bright colors
would scare away
their enemies.

But people don't always want
to scare away others.
Sometimes they paint their faces
to celebrate special days,
and sometimes
they paint their faces every day
because they believe
the paint makes them beautiful.

WHO AM I?

If you wear a mask,
you can look like
a snarling tiger,
a ferocious demon,
a snorting dragon,
or a funny clown.

If you wear a mask,
you can make people
frightened or happy,
and make them wonder
who you really are.

And if you don't tell anyone
who you are,
they will never know.
To find out, they would
have to peek
under your mask.

People use masks
to celebrate holidays,
and some even use them
to chase away evil spirits.

PICTURES ON THEIR SKIN

People usually put pictures
on paper, cloth, or wood.
But some people even put pictures
on their skin.
These pictures
are called tattoos.

A sailor from almost any land
might have a flag,
or an anchor,
or a ship
tattooed on his arm or chest.

In the South Sea Islands,
you can see people
with tattoos
from head to toe.

In Africa, some people
don't wear real necklaces,
but they tattoo pictures
of necklaces around their necks.

SPAIN

JAPAN

WAYS
TO
WEAR
HAIR

People in different lands
decorate their hair
in many different ways.
They decorate their hair
to celebrate holidays,
or to make themselves
look beautiful,
or sometimes just to do
what other people do.
They may knot their hair,
or snip it,
or curl it,
or fluff it.
They may braid their hair,
or roll it,
or tie it,
or color it.
They may even wave their hair
or twirl it.

Some people
decorate their hair with combs,
or pins,
or ribbons,
or beads,
or feathers,
or even bones.
And some people
even decorate their heads
by shaving off their hair!

HOLLAND

BURMA

THINGS
FOR
NOSES
AND
EARS

You wouldn't want
to wear a feather
in your nose.
It would tickle,
and it might make you sneeze.

But some Indians
are used to wearing
feathers in their noses,
so they don't sneeze at all.

A feather in your ear
would tickle, too.
But some American Indians
wear feathers in their ears
instead of earrings.

Some people wear other things
in their noses or ears.
Some wear rings.
Some wear shells.
Some wear stones.
Some wear sticks.
And some even wear bones
to decorate themselves
for special days,
or to make themselves beautiful.

INDIAN GIRL IN PANAMA

TRIBESMAN IN UGANDA

INDIAN IN AMAZONIAN JUNGLE

303

GIRLS IN KENYA

Ribbons and Medals

You couldn't walk if you wore all the different kinds of medals there are in the world. You probably couldn't even stand up because the medals would be so heavy.

Some soldiers win a lot of medals when they are brave, or loyal, or have been in special battles, or have fought in certain places. But, usually, they don't wear all their jangling medals. They wear ribbons that stand for the medals instead. Right above the coat pocket of their dress uniform they wear ribbons of red, or blue, or yellow, or white, or purple, or green, or almost any other color.

Some ribbons are striped and some are plain. The more ribbons a soldier wears, the more medals he has won.

Many other people who wear uniforms—sailors, pilots, firemen, and policemen—win medals and ribbons, too.

What Is a Totem Pole?

About the only place you can see
a fox sitting on a bear
with a beaver sitting on the fox
and an eagle sitting on the beaver
and a fish sitting on the eagle
is on a totem pole.

Of course, the animals are not real foxes,
bears, beavers, eagles, and fish.
They are carved out of a tall tree trunk
to make a totem pole.
Some totem poles have other animals carved on them.
Sometimes you might even see
the face of a man at the top!

A long time ago, tribes of Indians,
prayed to the animals that they carved
on their totem poles
for help and protection.

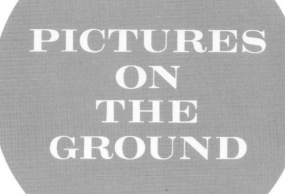

PICTURES
ON
THE
GROUND

It's time to take your medicine!
It's not in a spoon,
and it's not in a pill.
It's in a picture
on the ground.

In the United States,
special Indians
called medicine men
used to make pictures
on the ground with colored sand.
The medicine men thought
the picture on the ground
would be seen by the spirits,
and that they would help
a sick person get well.

Indians of India make pictures
on the ground, too.
But they don't use sand.
They use flour instead.
Every autumn, people who celebrate
the Divali Festival
make flour pictures
on their porches and doorsteps.

HANG THINGS ON MY BRANCHES

No matter where in the world I am,
people hang things on me.

In Lithuania,
they hang circles, squares,
and triangles of straw.

In Germany,
they decorate me
with cookies, apples, and oranges.

In the Ukraine,
they decorate me
with eggs and chains of paper.

In Japan,
they hang
tangerines and rice cookies
that tell your fortune.

But in the United States,
people decorate me
with things from many countries
because people
in the United States have come
from many parts
of the world.

I am a Christmas tree!

311

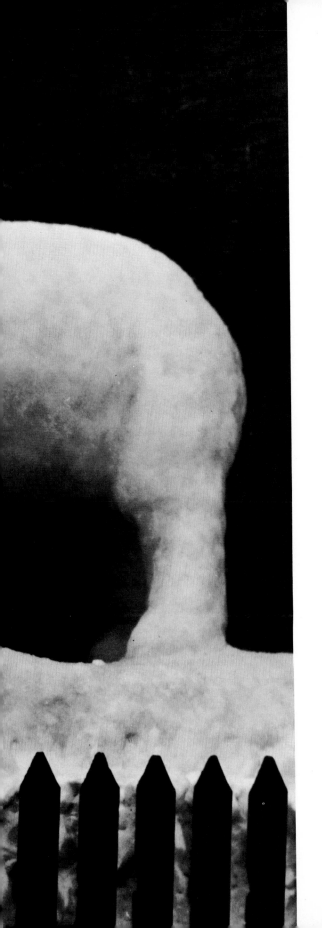

STATUES
THAT
MELT

A locomotive
that doesn't puff smoke,
an airplane
that can't fly,
and a grizzly bear
that can't scamper up a tree
are things you can see
at the Winter Carnival in Canada.

Every year
before Lent begins
the people have a contest
to see who can make
the best ice statue.

To make an ice statue,
first you make
a big pile of snow
and sprinkle it
with water.
As soon as the pile of snow
has turned into ice,
you are ready to carve it.

You take a small axe
and carve the ice
into whatever shape
you want it to be.

But after all that work,
warm weather comes
and your statue melts away.

313

Easter-Time Magic

You can be a magician! Maybe you can't make an elephant disappear, but you can make an egg change its color.

All you need is a bowl, a cloth, and dye. There are no strings or mirrors. And there is nothing up your sleeves.

All you do is put the dye into the bowl and wrap the egg in the cloth. Then dip the egg into the dye, swish it around, and pull it out. PRESTO—a colored Easter egg.

Or you can take more time—often many days—and paint beautiful pictures and designs on your Easter eggs, the way people do in Russia, Poland, and some other countries in Europe.

WAYS OF WORSHIP

People have many different ways
to worship.
People worship in churches,
in temples,
at shrines,
and some even pray
on a special rug.

The buildings where
people worship
are different, too.
Some have stained-glass windows.
Some of the floors are built
in the shape of a cross.
And some even have giants
and ogres at the door.

WINDOWS OF STAINED GLASS

In a church
you may see
windows that look
like big picture puzzles.

The windows are made
of many pieces
of colored glass.
The pieces of glass
usually are held together
with lead.

The windows are called
stained-glass windows.
They let light in
and they decorate the church.
Many stained-glass windows
show scenes
from stories
in the Bible.

GIANTS, DEMONS, AND DOGS OF STONE

How would you like
to come home
and find a giant,
or a demon,
or a huge stone dog
guarding your front door?

Statues of giants,
demons, and stone dogs
are used to guard temples
in China and Burma.
People there believe
that these fierce-looking
giants, demons, and animals
help to chase
evil spirits away.

In Europe,
ferocious stone demons,
called gargoyles,
sit on the edges
of church roofs.
Many are used
as waterspouts.
When it rains, the water
runs down the roof
and then pours
out the mouths
of the gargoyles.

BUDDHA OF KAMAKURA

Talking Statues

BUDDHA PREACHING A SERMON

Some statues just sit
and some just stand,
but some statues tell
something with their hands.

In Japan, you can see
that the hands
on many statues are held
in different ways.

BUDDHA TEACHING

The hands
of the Buddha of Kamakura
mean that he is praying.

The hands
of another Buddha statue
show that anyone can learn
what Buddha taught,
if they try hard enough.

The hands
of still another
Buddha statue show
that he is
conquering demons.

BUDDHA CONQUERING DEMONS

In other statues,
Buddha holds his hands
in different ways
to say different things.

321

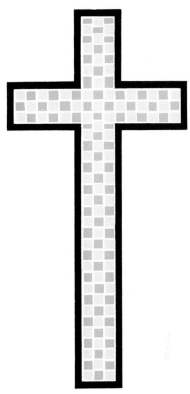

CROSSES
AND
STARS

You can see a cross on
the steeple,
the walls,
and the altar
of many churches.

Even the floors
of some churches
are built in the shape
of a cross.

But you do not always
see a cross
where people worship.
At a Jewish synagogue
you would see
a star with six points.
It is the Star of David.

And on an Islamic mosque
you would see a star
with a crescent.

323

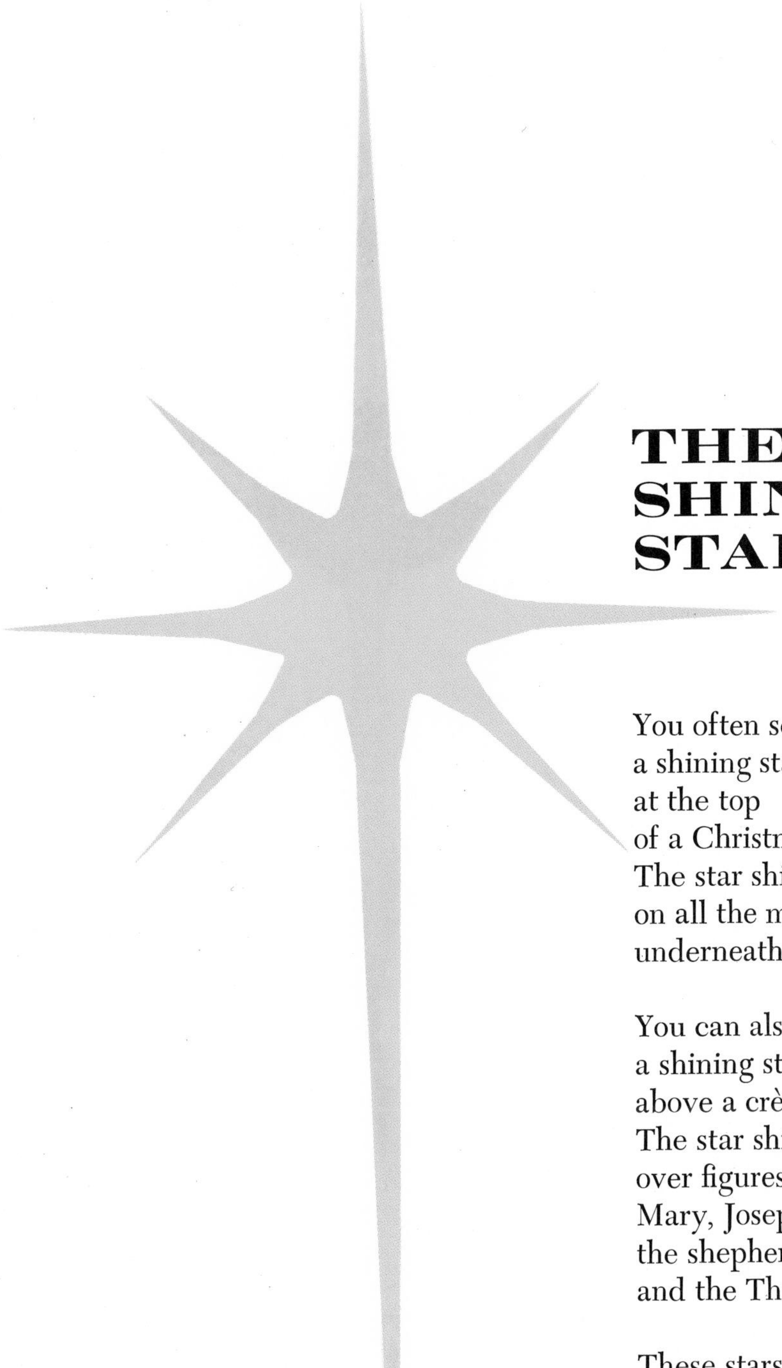

THE
SHINING
STAR

You often see
a shining star
at the top
of a Christmas tree.
The star shines down
on all the mysterious packages
underneath the tree.

You can also see
a shining star
above a crèche.
The star shines
over figures of Jesus,
Mary, Joseph,
the shepherds,
and the Three Wise Men.

These stars
are supposed to be
like the one
that led the Wise Men
to Jesus.

PRAYER RUGS

There are rugs
to walk on
and there are rugs
to pray on.

Moslems are people
who follow a religion
called Islam.
They kneel on a special rug
when they pray.

A Moslem usually has
his prayer rug
rolled up
ready to use.
Every morning,
noon,
afternoon,
evening,
and night
he unrolls his rug
and kneels on it to pray.

MUEZZINS AND BELLS

Dong,
dong,
d-o-n-g—
the church bells
ring out.

In many countries,
such as the United States,
England, and France,
church bells ring
to call people to worship
on Sunday morning.

But in some countries,
like Turkey, Iraq, and Iran,
there are no bells
to call people to worship.
Instead, there are men
called muezzins.

A muezzin stands
in a tall tower
called a minaret.
Five times a day
the muezzin climbs to the top
of the minaret and chants
the call to worship
as loudly as he can
to the people below.

EASTER LILY
AND PALM

Lilies of white
and palms of green
mean Easter time
in the United States.

Each year people
decorate their churches
with lilies and palms
to celebrate
the resurrection of Jesus.
Some people believe
that the palm means peace
and that the lily means
beauty and goodness.

CARL YATES

RELIGIOUS CHRISTMAS CARDS

There are long cards,
tiny cards,
shiny cards,
and sparkling cards.

Some Christmas cards show
snowmen, candles, and holly.
Some show Christmas trees
and Santa Claus.
But other Christmas cards show
the real meaning of Christmas—
the celebration of the birth of Jesus.

Some of these cards show
pictures of the Three Wise Men
on their camels,
Jesus in a manger,
or Jesus in the arms of his mother.
These are called Nativity scenes.

DAYS OF THANKSGIVING

What day would it be if you were eating a steaming turkey, bright red cranberries, and a pumpkin pie? In the United States, it would be Thanksgiving Day.

What day would it be if you went to a church that was decorated with sheaves of oats, apples and pears, and vegetables of green? In England, it would be Harvest Home Day.

What day would it be if you bowed before a shrine of candles and offered a bowl of rice? In Japan, it would be a harvest festival day.

These all are days of thanksgiving that come in the fall, when people in many different countries pray and give thanks for the food that they eat.

SACRED COWS AND MONKEYS

Why would a cow
be walking through a store?
Why would a monkey
be riding on a bus?

In India, people
let cows and monkeys
do anything.
Some people believe
that cows and monkeys
are sacred animals
and that no one
should hurt them.

The animals come and go
wherever they want to.
Sometimes they even
go to sleep
in the middle of the street.
Some people bow
to the cows
when they pass them.

The monkeys
even have special temples
where they live and eat
all the peanuts they want.

POURING
TEA
ON AN
ELEPHANT

An elephant,
pink flowers,
and sweet tea
are the things
that are used
for a special birthday
in Japan.

Every year in April
some Japanese children
celebrate the birthday
of Buddha.
Sometimes they celebrate
with a large elephant
that is made
of papier-mâché
and painted red and white.
On the elephant's back
is a small house
covered with pink flowers.

Inside the house
is a statue of Buddha.
The children walk
up to the statue
and bow and pour
sweet tea on its head.
Some people believe
that on the day
Buddha was born
it rained tea
instead of water.

Jewish children have a celebration called Hanukkah. It usually comes in the same month as Christmas.

Hanukkah lasts for eight days. Every night the family gathers to light special candles and say special prayers. Then the children sing with their parents.

The candles are set in a candleholder called a menorah. On the first night, one candle is set in the menorah and lighted. Each night another candle is added and lighted.

On the last night of Hanukkah, eight burning candles stand in the menorah. One candle is for each night of the celebration.

Hanukkah is an old celebration. Long ago, the Jewish people won back the temple in Jerusalem that had been taken away from them. They built a new altar and lighted a new fire. Legend says there was only enough oil for the fire to last one day. But the oil burned for eight days.

Today, Hanukkah is a way of remembering the victory. It is also a time when the children get presents on each day of the celebration.

Another time the children celebrate is Rosh Hashanah, the Jewish New Year. Rosh Hashanah comes in September or October.

8 candles,

8 days

THE TORII

When you sail out to sea,
people in Japan say
that you can bring your boat
good luck by sailing
under a torii.

A torii
is made of logs
and painted
with bright colors.

A torii can also be
a gateway
to a Shinto temple.
Sometimes
instead of going
under just one torii,
you must pass under
many of them.

Today's Pilgrims

Would you believe it if you saw a house floating through the air? Some people believe that is just what happened to a special house in Italy. And, they believe that the house seemed to be floating, because angels were carrying it. Today, that house is a church in a city called Loreto. Every year people come from near and far to see it, because they believe that it is a holy place. When they do, we say that they are making a pilgrimage.

In India, other people make pilgrimages to a river called the Ganges. They believe that the Ganges is a sacred river that flows straight to heaven.

In Saudi Arabia, other people make pilgrimages to see a special black stone in a city called Mecca. They believe that the Black Stone is sacred and that it came from heaven.

In many parts of the world, you might see people making pilgrimages to places that they believe are holy.

PILGRIMS VISIT THE SHRINE AT LOURDES, FRANCE.

344

STORIES OF FAVORITE HOLIDAYS

If you had lived
long, long ago,
you could have seen
the first time
some favorite holidays
were celebrated.

You could have seen shepherds
looking for a baby.
You could have seen a lady
placing flowers
on the graves
of soldiers.
You could have seen a man
discovering North America.

You can find out
which favorite holidays
they were—and still are—
when you read
the pages that follow.

The First Christmas

What did a doctor named Luke
have to do with the story
of the first Christmas?
He was one of the few men
who wrote about it in the Bible.
Luke wrote that long ago,
an angel appeared to shepherds
in the fields outside
the little town of Bethlehem.
The angel told the shepherds about
a special baby born that day.
The baby was the Christ Child,
and the shepherds found Him
in a place where cattle lived.
He was wrapped in long strips of cloth,
called swaddling clothes,
and He lay in a manger filled with straw.
Those shepherds and other people called
Christians believe that the baby
was the Son of God.

The birthday of the Christ Child
was celebrated at different times
until a Roman bishop declared
that Christmas should be celebrated
on December 25. And that's the day when
Christmas has been celebrated ever since.

"THE NATIVITY," A MOSAIC IN PALATINE CHAPEL, PALERMO, ITALY

GEORGE WASHINGTON AND HIS ARMY DURING THE REVOLUTIONARY WAR.

Birthdays of Presidents

If you belong to a club, you have a leader. If the leader is you, you're something like the president of a country.

Long ago, before there was a country called the United States, there were 13 states called colonies. When the colonies decided to become the United States, they needed a leader. So they voted for George Washington who became their first President.

Washington had no idea that the nation's capital would be named after him. He had no idea that in the capital there would be a tall monument that honors him as the "Father of His Country." He had no idea that his birthday, on February 22, would become a legal holiday.

Someday when you grow up, you might become the leader of your country. And who knows? Then maybe your birthday might become a legal holiday, too!

The Other Side of a Penny

If you have a certain kind of penny, you have clues about a certain holiday in February. On one side of the penny, you can see a picture of the man whose birthday, February 12, is a holiday in many parts of the United States. Do you know who this man was?

He was born in a log cabin in Kentucky. When he grew up, he became a lawyer. Later, he became the sixteenth President of the United States. One evening, he went to the theater with his wife and was shot.

Turn the penny over, and you will see a picture of the building that was built in Washington, D. C., to honor this man. If you look closely at the picture of the building on the penny, you can even see the statue of this man. The building is the Lincoln Memorial, and it honors Abraham Lincoln, the man whose birthday is celebrated on February 12.

LINCOLN MEMORIAL, WASHINGTON, D. C.

Flowers, Flags, and Wreaths

Did you ever wear a bright red poppy made of cloth? Some people do on or close to Memorial Day in May. The poppy is worn in memory of those who died in wars.

It is said that the idea for Memorial Day happened during the Civil War, or the War Between the States. On May 30, a Frenchwoman, Cassandra Oliver Moncure, who lived in the South, placed fresh flowers on the graves of soldiers. Maybe she chose the 30th of May because she remembered that is was the day the people of France honored one of their greatest leaders, Napoleon Bonaparte.

Since then, Memorial Day is a day when people in the United States have a holiday from school and work so that they can honor those who died in wars. They may watch parades. They may wear a bright red poppy made of cloth. And, they may decorate graves with flowers, flags, or wreathes.

A SCENE FROM A MOVIE ABOUT THE CIVIL WAR IN THE UNITED STATES.

WORLD WAR I SOLDIERS PARADE IN NEW YORK CITY, 1919.

A Special Day for Veterans

If you know a soldier, a sailor, a marine, an airman, or anyone who went to war, you know a veteran. And all veterans who fought for the United States or Canada are honored by their countries on the 11th of November. In Canada, November 11 is now called "Remembrance Day." And in the United States, November 11 is called "Veterans Day."

Veterans Day and Remembrance Day used to be called Armistice Day. Armistice is a word that means that the countries that were at war have stopped fighting. During World War I, the fighting stopped on November 11. This was the first Armistice Day. For many years, the veterans of World War I were honored on that day. But then came other wars and other veterans. So Armistice Day became known as Veterans Day in the United States and Remembrance Day in Canada.

It's a day for parades, and speeches, and a moment of silence to think about the people who gave their lives in wars.

The Glorious Holiday

Do you know why some people in the United States shoot off fire-crackers and skyrockets on the Fourth of July? They're celebrating Independence Day—the birthday of the United States.

On July 4 in 1776, an important paper called the Declaration of Independence was signed. It told the world that the colonists in America had decided to unite. And once the people united, it was only 12 years later that the country called "the United States" got its name and Constitution.

But since it all began on July 4, 1776, no wonder Old Glory, the

A PAINTING CALLED "FOURTH OF JULY PARADE" BY ALFRED HOWLAND

American flag, flies from flagpoles all over the 50 states on Independence Day! No wonder the people celebrate with parades and picnics and fireworks!

Other countries celebrate their Independence Days, too. In Italy, it's called Anniversary of the Republic on June 2. In Canada, it's called Dominion Day on July 1. In France, it's called Bastille Day on July 14.

Wherever people live in a land that's free, Independence Day is a glorious holiday!

353

Columbus and Leif Ericson

You may call October 12 "Discovery Day" or "Landing Day." But most people in the United States call it Columbus Day. That's because Christopher Columbus reached the New World on October 12, 1492. He set sail from a country called Spain with three ships: the *Niña*, the *Pinta*, and the *Santa María*. Many people laughed at Columbus. They thought the world was flat. They thought Columbus and his ships would sail right off the edge into the Sea of Darkness. But Columbus proved that they were wrong.

In the United States there's a day for Leif Ericson, too—he's the one (not counting the Indians who were already there) who really discovered America. His day is October 9.

Leif Ericson's small boats reached the New World almost five hundred years before Columbus' three ships did.

But the funny thing about these two famous discoverers is that neither one knew what he had discovered.

A PAINTING CALLED "COLUMBUS DISCOVERS AMERICA" BY N. C. WYETH

Snowdrops, Hearts, and Cupids

How would you like to find a pressed snowdrop inside an envelope on Saint Valentine's Day? The "snowdrop" isn't the kind of snow that drifts down from the sky, but the name of a flower that grows in many parts of the world. That's the kind of valentine that young people in Denmark send on February 14.

But in England, France, Canada, and the United States, people send cards decorated with hearts and flowers and cupids. The cards are called valentines. Some valentines have funny pictures and jokelike verses. We call these *comic* valentines.

Valentines are named after a good man who lived long ago, more years ago than anybody can remember. Some people believe that he helped to make a blind girl see. He was put to death on February 14, and his church chose this day to honor him. Long before Saint Valentine lived, and ever since he died, February 14 has been a day for letting others know that they are special.

SAINT VALENTINE

357

Why Halloween?

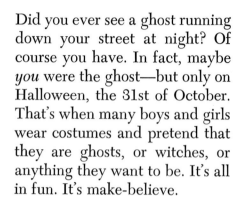

Did you ever see a ghost running down your street at night? Of course you have. In fact, maybe *you* were the ghost—but only on Halloween, the 31st of October. That's when many boys and girls wear costumes and pretend that they are ghosts, or witches, or anything they want to be. It's all in fun. It's make-believe.

But long ago, long before Halloween became Halloween, some people in Europe really believed that ghosts groaned and moaned as they roamed about on the last day of October. These superstitious people built bonfires to keep the ghosts away. Then they used the bonfires to cook a feast. They were celebrating the end of summer.

Later, the celebration day became known as Halloween. *Hallow* means "holy" and *e'en* is short for "evening." *Hallow een* is the evening before Allhallows Day, sometimes called All Saints' Day.

Halloween is a favorite holiday for children in Canada and the United States. It's also celebrated in England and Ireland.

ANCIENT DRUIDS AROUND A BONFIRE ON THE EVENING OF OCTOBER 31ST.

A Calendar of

Celebration Days

YOU CAN READ MORE ABOUT THESE DAYS IN THIS BOOK

Illustration
Acknowledgments

The publishers of CHILDCRAFT gratefully acknowledge the courtesy of the following artists, photographers, publishers, agencies, and corporations for illustrations in this volume. Page numbers refer to two-page spreads. The words "(*left*)," "(*center*)," "(*top*)," "(*bottom*)," and "(*right*)," indicate position on the spread. All illustrations are the exclusive property of the publishers of CHILDCRAFT unless names are marked with an asterisk (*).

INTRODUCTION:
4–6: Dean Wessel

COSTUMES FOR SPECIAL DAYS:
7: Dean Wessel
8–9: George Suyeoka
10–11: (*left*) courtesy of Ciba Limited, Basle, Switzerland (*); (*right*) Karl Gullers, Rapho-Guillumette (*)
12–13: Dean Wessel
14–15: Carl Yates
16–17: George Suyeoka
18–19: Camera Press, Pix (*)
20–21: Belgian National Tourist Office (*)
22–23: photo, Swiss National Tourist Office (*); art by Nita Engel—Hollis Studio
24–25: George Suyeoka
26–27: Dean Wessel
28–29: Don Almquist
30–31: Herbert Danska
32: Swiss National Tourist Office (*)

CLOTHES IN MANY LANDS:
33: Dean Wessel
34–35: (*left*) United States Navy (*); (*right*) Don Taka
36–37: art by Don Almquist; photos, (*left to right*) Fredrick Ayers III, Photo Researchers (*), Robert Doisneau, Rapho-Guillumette (*), Gunther Reitz, Pix (*), Charles Trieschmann, Black Star (*), E. R. Moore Co. (*)
38–39: (*left*) Ben McCall, FPG (*); (*right*) John Titchen, Photo-Library
40–41: Herbert Danska
42–43: Don Almquist
44–45: William Gorman—Stevens-Gross Studios, Inc.
46–47: art by Herbert Danska; photos, (*top to bottom*) Don Stebbing, Richard Harrington, Three Lions (*), Photo-Library for CHILDCRAFT
48–49: art by Herbert Danska; photos, (*left*) Philip Gendreau (*), (*right*) CHILDCRAFT photo
50: Japan National Tourist Association (*)

FLAGS:
51: Dean Wessel
52–53: Joseph Pearson
54–55: Carl Yates
56–57: art by Georges Michel—Stevens-Gross Studios, Inc.; photo, Ewing Galloway (*)
58–59: Georges Michel—Stevens-Gross Studios, Inc.
60–61: Joseph Pearson
62: Japan National Tourist Association (*)

FIREWORKS, FIRES, AND CANDLES:
63: Dean Wessel
64–65: Mary Horton
66–67: art by Carl Yates; photo, Lyons, Photo-Library (*)
68–69: Carl Yates

70–71: art by Robert Borja; photo, Chinese News Service (*)
72–73: French Embassy Press & Information Division (*)
74–75: Bill Hammond
76–77: Roy Andersen
78–79: Dave Blossom
80–81: Frank M. Walsh, Photo-Library (*)
82: Gurney Miller

GIVING AND GETTING GIFTS:
83: Dean Wessel
84–85: Don Almquist
86–87: art by Nita Engel—Hollis Studio; photo, German Information Center (*)
88–89: Suzi Hawes and Mary Horton
90–91: Mary Horton
92–93: Mary Horton
94–95: Don Almquist
96–97: Sidney Rafilson
98: Robert Boehmer

TRICKS AND GAMES FOR SPECIAL DAYS:
99: Dean Wessel
100–101: George Suyeoka
102–103: George Suyeoka
104–105: George Pickow, Three Lions (*)
106–107: Comet, Zurich from Swiss National Tourist Office (*)
108–109: art by George Suyeoka; photo, West Virginia Industrial and Publicity Commission (*)
110–111: Mary Horton
112–113: Mary Horton
114–115: art by George Suyeoka; photo, Oregon State Highway Department (*)
116–117: Thomson Newspapers Limited, London (*)
118: Robert Davis (*)

GAMES THE WORLD OVER:
191: Dean Wessel
120–121: Luke Doheny—Visual Art Studios, Inc.
122–123: Luke Doheny—Visual Art Studios, Inc.
124–125: Luke Doheny—Visual Art Studios, Inc.
126–127: Luke Doheny—Visual Art Studios, Inc.
128–129: Luke Doheny—Visual Art Studios, Inc.
130–131: Luke Doheny—Visual Art Studios, Inc.
132: Don Stebbing

TOYS WHEREVER YOU GO:
133: Dean Wessel
134–135: photo, Fuji Service & Trading Co., Tokyo (*); art by Carl Martin—Business Arts, Inc.
136–137: (*left*) Gordon Brusstar; (*right*) Paul McNear
138–139: art by John M. Bolt, Jr.; photo by Don Stebbing
140–141: Robert Kresin
142–143: (*left*) Arizona Photographic Associates (*); (*top right*) Don Stebbing; (*bottom right*) H. Armstrong Roberts (*)

Index to Volume 5

This index is designed so that you can easily find any holiday or custom. There are entries for specific holidays, customs, countries, and other special topics. For example, to find out about Christmas in France, look up Christmas, France; or France, Christmas. You can also look up such subjects as, Père Noël; Shoes, wooden; or Cake of the Kings. To find out about food in different countries, look up the entry Food customs or look up the specific country. A general index to CHILDCRAFT appears in Volume 15.